FORERUNNERS: IDEAS FIRST FROM THE UNIVERSITY OF
MINNESOTA PRESS

Original e-works to spark new scholarship

FORERUNNERS: IDEAS FIRST is a thought-in-process series of break-
through digital works. Written between fresh ideas and finished books,
Forerunners draws on scholarly work initiated in notable blogs, social
media, conference plenaries, journal articles, and the synergy of academic exchange. This is gray literature publishing: where intense
thinking, change, and speculation take place in scholarship.

A Third University Is Possible

A Third University Is Possible

la paperson

University of Minnesota Press

MINNEAPOLIS

Published by the University of Minnesota Press, 2017
111 Third Avenue South, Suite 290
Minneapolis, MN 55401-2520
http://www.upress.umn.edu

The University of Minnesota is an equal-opportunity educator and employer.

For you, who are the business

Even when they are dangerous
examine the heart of those machines you hate
before you discard them

—AUDRE LORDE

Contents

Introduction

WITHIN THE COLONIZING UNIVERSITY also exists a decolonizing education. Occupying the same space and time are the colonizer's territories and institutions and colonized time, but also Indigenous land and life before and beyond occupation. Colonial schools are machines running on desires for a colonizer's future and, paradoxically, desires for Indigenous futures. In this respect, paraphrasing the words of Linda Tuhiwai Smith, the present of school is permeable to the time now (colonization), the time before that (precolonial), and the time beyond of all of that (decolonial).[1] Regardless of its colonial structure, because school is an assemblage of machines and not a monolithic institution, its machinery is always being subverted toward decolonizing purposes. The bits of machinery that make up a decolonizing university are driven by decolonial desires, with decolonizing dreamers who are subversively part of the machinery and part machine themselves. These subversive beings wreck, scavenge, retool, and reassemble the colonizing university into decolonizing contraptions. They are scyborgs with a decolonizing desire. You might choose to be one of them.

1. Linda Tuhiwai Smith, *Decolonizing Methodologies: Research and Indigenous Peoples* (New York: St Martin's Press, 1999).

Scyborg—composed of *s + cyborg*—is a queer turn of word that I offer to you to name the structural agency of persons who have picked up colonial technologies and reassembled them to decolonizing purposes. Foundational femtech theorists have used *cyborg*, that is, the "cybernetic organism" with new or restored abilities through integration with technological components, to destabilize how we think of the human body as a discrete corporeal entity, to disrupt essentialisms as described by the binary of artificial–spiritual identities, and to challenge how we think of the agency of objects and apparatuses.[2] However, whereas cyborg theory highlighted the technological nature of the body, the scyborg is not preoccupied with debates about hir machine–organic nature. Rather, the scyborg delights in the ways that hir agency is extended by the very circuitry of systems meant to colonize. Scyborg is system-interference and system-witchcraft, the ghost in the machine. Like a mutant code, scyborg is structure's agency in a nonstandard deviation. Scyborg's silent addition begs the question of what it is: a Scylla or a Scully, an alternative spelling, a plurality, or an assemblage, a slippage between cyborg and system? I mean for you to apply this term to yourself.[3] I hope you have fun with it. And also build a decolonizing machine while you're at it. For you, who likes to create a mess out of colonial apparatuses.

This short book insists on the possibilities for a third world university committed to the practical work of decolonization. I frame the university broadly as an amalgamation of first, second, and third *worlding* formations. That is, the university is world-*making*. First worlding universities are machinery commissioned

2. Donna Jeanne Haraway, *Simians, Cyborgs, and Women: The Reinvention of Nature* (New York: Routledge, 1991); Karen Barad, "Getting Real: Technoscientific Practices and the Materialization of Reality," *Differences: A Journal of Feminist Cultural Studies* 10, no. 2 (1998): 87–128; see also Jasbir K. Puar, "'I Would Rather Be a Cyborg than a Goddess': Becoming-Intersectional in Assemblage Theory," *PhiloSOPHIA* 2, no. 1 (2012): 49–66.

3. Anyway, you might prefer it to *cyborg*.

to actualize imperialist dreams of a settled world. Second worlding universities desire to humanize the world, which is a more
genteel way to colonize a world that is so much more than human. A third worlding university is a decolonizing university. This
frame helps us assess the academic–industrial complex with its
current neoliberal machinery and its investments in colonialism,
but more importantly, it is a frame that describes the decolonial
desires that already inhabit and repurpose the academic machinery.[4] Decolonization is, put bluntly, the rematriation of land, the
regeneration of relations, and the forwarding of Indigenous and
Black and queer futures—a process that requires countering what
power seems to be up to. To take effective decolonizing action, we
must then have a theory of action that accounts for the perme-
ability of the apparatuses of power and the fact that neocolonial
systems inadvertently support decolonizing agendas. This manuscript presents a theory of action in assemblage: the scyborg. Or
more precisely, the scyborg is a theory of assemblage in action, of
a structural agency that produces the third world university. The
third world university is multiscalar; that is, it is transnational in
scope, with a multitude of campuses, yet locally specific to address
decolonization in its particularities. Its scope is at the scale of the
apparatus and at the scale of the personal; its temporalities are
transhistorical and futuristic. It already exists.

Colonial schools have a tradition of harboring spaces of anticolonial resistance. These contradictions are exquisitely written
about by the eminent novelist, literary scholar, and postcolonial
thinker Ngũgĩ wa Thiong'o. He describes how the machine of
British colonial schooling in Kenya produced a Black governor

4. I use *third university* and *third world university* interchangeably as
shorthand for a third worlding university, that is, a decolonizing university.
Readers might find *third world university* easier to say aloud. The fourth
world university refers to something else entirely outside of this taxonomy
of universities. These terms are not meant to be categorical. Universities are
permeable and coinciding.

of colonial Kenya and, paradoxically, also helped to produce Mau
Mau revolutionaries. Fearful that schools sheltered the Mau Mau,
who occupied the imaginations of Indigenous Kenyans and settlers alike as the quintessential Black, violent resistance movement, the colonial state banned many of its missionary-inspired
schools in the 1952 declaration of a state of emergency. This ban
included the Kenya Teachers College, whose campus was converted into "a prison camp where proponents of resistance to colonialism were hanged."[5] During the Mau Mau Rebellion, wa Thiong'o
attended Alliance High School, a segregated, elite missionary
school for Black Africans in British Kenya. And prior to that, he
attended Manguo elementary school, which was banned for a time
by the colonial government. How can colonial schools become disloyal to colonialism? According to wa Thiong'o, the decolonial is
always already amid the colonial.

Colonial schools have been trafficked around the world.
Colonial schooling in Kenya, Black schooling in the post-Abolition
U.S. South, education for pacification of Indigenous peoples in
the Pacific, and Indian boarding schools in North America are en-
twined through a set of exchanges of people, ideas, models, and
philosophies never more than a few degrees of separation from
the U.S. Department of War. Kenya's Alliance High School was
"modeled on the nineteenth-century system for educating Native
Americans and African Americans in the South." In 1924–25,
G. A. Grieves, the first principal of Alliance, visited and studied "the
Virginia Hampton Institute, founded in 1868 by General Samuel C.
Armstrong, the son of a missionary in Hawai'i, and Tuskegee
Institute, founded in 1881 by Booker T. Washington, a graduate of
Hampton and protégé of Armstrong."[6] Designed to educate Black
Americans in the U.S. South, Hampton and Tuskegee were the

5. Ngũgĩ wa Thiong'o, *Dreams in a Time of War: A Childhood Memoir*
(New York: Pantheon Books, 2010), 166.

6. Ngũgĩ wa Thiong'o, *In the House of the Interpreter: A Memoir* (New
York: Pantheon Books, 2012), 10.

models for colonial schools implemented throughout the world. These include the total public school system built and run by the U.S. Army in the Philippines beginning in 1901, a military appropriation according to General Arthur MacArthur necessary "as an adjunct to military operations calculated to pacify the people."[7] They include the Carlisle Indian boarding school founded by Captain "kill-the-Indian-save-the-man" Pratt in 1879. In these global lines of flight—missions in the Kingdom of Hawai'i, American Indian boarding schools, "Negro uplift" schools in the South, segregated elite Black schooling in British Kenya, U.S. Army–run schools in the Philippines—we have a map of the trafficking of colonial technologies in radically different lands.

Yet colonial schools carry decolonial riders. Like all colonial technologies, "this system did not always produce the intended result."[8] Colonial schools are especially geared to contradictory desires: the production of "self-reliant" Blacks and the pacification of their political dissidence in the case of Alliance. Booker T. Washington's idea of self-reliance was in no small part used to quell Black, Native, or, in the case of Kenya, Black Native unrest by developing a middle class of public servants to collaborate with the colonialist government. Yet Washington's self-reliance also informed radical imaginations, such as Marcus Garvey's pan-Africanism and Black economic sovereignty. Carter G. Woodson, noted founder of Black History Month and author of *The Miseducation of the Negro* (1933), attended the segregated Douglass School in post-Reconstruction Virginia (home to the Hampton Institute). A lesser-known de/colonial connection is that Woodson worked as a teacher, then as school supervisor, for the U.S. Army schools in the Philippines from 1903 to 1907. His book became the

7. Arthur MacArthur, cited in Renato Constantino, "The Miseducation of the Filipino," *Weekly Graphic,* June 8, 1966, 3. Internet resource transcribed by Bert M. Drona, *The Filipino Mind,* http://thefilipinomind.blogspot.com/.

8. Wa Thiong'o, *In the House of the Interpreter,* 10.

critical referent for Renato Constantino's "The Miseducation of the Filipino" (1966). Taking off from the colonial landing are always already decolonial lines of flight, or the "witch's flight," an uncanny turn of phrase that Kara Keeling reinvents to describe the transgressive path of the Black Femme.

Keeling explores the Black Femme in cinema, and in society, because her treatment of the cinematic is less about representation and more about the cinematic production of reality (following Gilles Deleuze). The Black Femme is violently pushed aside in commonsense notions of radical Black politics, an effect that is clear in the visual field of Hollywood-made films for/about Black people. Nonetheless, the Black Femme is there, appearing and then disappearing to the offscreen world. Just beyond the frame, she is a "seething spectral presence" that disrupts the common sense of hegemonic Black masculinity and attendant forms of Black womanhood that have become the metonyms for Black radical politics and revolutionary change. In this respect, the Black Femme is a spectral figure, who when followed, leads us to "a more radical elsewhere"—a world just beyond the frame, with imaginaries of justice and gender and ways of being-in-community that are alternatives from the cinematic common sense. This movement off the screen, out of the frame of dominant common sense, is the witch's flight.[9]

I hear the rustle of the witch's flight in Scott Lyons's witty and insightful reflections on Indian boarding schools and the American Indian Movement (AIM). He describes his grandfather's experiences of running away three times from an off-reservation boarding school, for which he was "cruelly whipped with a leather strap in front of a school assembly," prompting his fourth and final es-

9. Avery Gordon, *Ghostly Matters: Haunting and the Sociological Imagination* (Minneapolis: University of Minnesota Press, 2008), 18; Kara Keeling, *The Witch's Flight: The Cinematic, the Black Femme, and the Image of Common Sense,* Perverse Modernities (Durham, N.C.: Duke University Press, 2007), 137.

cape, never to return. In relating his grandfather's boarding school story, Lyons acknowledges the importance of such grim narratives in constituting a necessary critical discourse about boarding schools as a part of a policy of cultural genocide. However, he points out that inventive paths through boarding schools might be overlooked when we only narrate an overdetermined critique of settler schooling:

> All of us grandkids interviewed [my grandfather Aub] for paper assignments at one point or another, and we always did well on our papers. No one ever wanted to interview Aub's wife, my Dakota grandmother from the Lower Sioux Indian Community (Morton), who attended the same school ten years after my grandfather, and loved it completely.... My grandmother was the first in my line to receive not only a high school diploma—she graduated valedictorian—but also the first higher education, attending a teacher's college and eventually becoming one of Leech Lake's first Indian teachers.[10]

Lyons credits his grandmother for the education of his generation of cousins, a reality made possible by his grandmother's different line of flight from school. In yet another divergent set of tracks through school, AIM and Red Power activists eventually occupied Lyons's old Head Start classroom. Like wa Thiong'o, Lyons's relationship to revolution was complex. His grandparents scorned the "AIMsters," while Lyons secretly adored "those young Indians with their long hair and horses—also guns."[11] Despite being its biopolitical target, Indigenous people ride the currents of school in surprising directions.

Drawing from the Hopi concept of footprint or "track" as metaphorical/metaphysical trails through the sacred landscape, K. Tsianina Lomawaima and Teresa McCarty draw our attention to the possibilities created by and through Native tracking over

---

10. Scott Richard Lyons, *X-Marks: Native Signatures of Assent,* Indigenous Americas (Minneapolis: University of Minnesota Press, 2010), 23.

11. Ibid., 31.

a hundred years of schooling. "We search for the footprints of Native presence in a century of American Indian education, looking for the unexpected, the overlooked, the seemingly paradoxical results of and responses to domineering policies and institutions."[12] While maintaining a sharp critique of the curriculum of cultural genocide in the design of Indian education, they dispose of the overdetermined critique of Indian schools as simply a reflex and robot of their settler colonial masters. Instead, they look at the Hopification of settler schooling, "the age-old process of Hopi people learning and adapting from others useful ideas, practices, technologies, and material culture."[13] For me, their work emphasizes how Hopification is futuristic—both in terms of Hopi technological adaptations and, more importantly, because Hopi reassemblages bear into existence a Hopi future. For example, Lomawaima and McCarty detail the decolonial elements written into the educational readers, printed and distributed and assigned by the U.S. federal government. Someone's hand wrote those readers and, furthermore, bent the apparatus of printing, distribution, and official curriculum. We have to keep in mind that printed readers are a technology, as are their systems of distribution. What we ought to find amazing in Lomawaima and McCarty's instructive work are the ways that technological apparatuses become subverted toward decolonization. Again, I feel the electrostatic discharge of the witch's flight.

There is no adequate English word for "beyond colonization." The best English-ish phrases that I have heard are Kale Fajardo's "trans*colonial" and "shadow sovereignty" as theorized by Native literary scholars.[14] For Craig Womack, sovereignty is more deep-

12. K. Tsianina Lomawaima and Teresa McCarty, *"To Remain an Indian": Lessons in Democracy from a Century of Native American Education,* Multicultural Education (New York: Teachers College Press, 2006), 13.

13. Ibid., 111. *Hopification* is Hartman H. Lomawaima's term. See Lomawaima, "Hopification: A Strategy for Cultural Preservation," *Columbian Consequences* 1 (1989): 93–99.

14. Kale Fajardo, "Filipino Goonies in Astoria, Oregon: Engaging

ly expressed in the dynamic language of literature than in the restrictive definitions of treaty law. In Womack's fictional writing, the tie-snakes are an underwater kingdom of monsters, "something white man has never saw or caught," that seem like a metaphor for a world beyond colonization.[15] Greg Sarris sums up this deeper sovereignty very simply: "It's not *like* anything."[16] Certainly *freedom* when spoken with an African diasporic accent gestures toward radical elsewheres, elusive destinations made possible by the very audacity to dream freedom.[17] Such words are already more than English. The word *postcolonial* is disappointing as far as bringing about decolonization and is at best shorthand for the

---

Settler Colonialisms in Queer/Asian Diaspora Studies and Transnational Filipino/a Studies," invited talk, Department of Ethnic Studies, University of California, San Diego, February 18, 2015; Greg Sarris, *Keeping Slug Woman Alive: A Holistic Approach to American Indian Texts* (Berkeley: University of California Press, 1993); Gerald Robert Vizenor, *Manifest Manners: Postindian Warriors of Survivance* (Hanover, N.H.: University Press of New England, 1994); Craig S. Womack, *Red on Red: Native American Literary Separatism* (Minneapolis: University of Minnesota Press, 1999); Troy Richardson, "Navigating the Problem of Inclusion as Enclosure in Native Culture–Based Education: Theorizing Shadow Curriculum," *Curriculum Inquiry* 41, no. 3 (2011): 332–49; Aries River Yumul, "Sovereignty's Shadow: How Queer Native American Co-constitutive Relations in Literature Rethink Space, Land, Healing, and Resistance," honors thesis, University of California, San Diego, 2012.

15. Craig S. Womack, *Drowning in Fire*, Sun Tracks 48 (Tucson: University of Arizona Press, 2001), 19.

16. Greg Sarris, *Watermelon Nights: A Novel*, 1st ed. (New York: Hyperion, 1998), 136.

17. Robin D. G. Kelley, *Freedom Dreams: The Black Radical Imagination* (Boston: Beacon Press, 2002). See also Shelley Streeby, "Speculative Archives: Histories of the Future of Education," *Pacific Coast Philology* 49, no. 1 (2014): 25–40, for a great analysis of Black and transborder utopian projects by Frederic Jameson, Kim Stanley Robinson, Octavia Butler, and Alex Rivera. Drawing from Kim Stanley Robinson's valuing on the very audacity to dream utopia, Streeby supplies an important refusal of heavy-handed critiques of utopia, such as my own in "The Postcolonial Ghetto: Seeing Her Shape and His Hand," *Berkeley Review of Education* 1, no. 1 (2010): 5–34.

complexities of contemporary colonial crap. I only find it useful when an awkward + glyph adds other meanings into it: the post+-colonial. Posts+ are the postings or updates on colonialism, the posts or appointed roles within colonizing institutions, the outposts where colonial force needs fortification—but also the post-scripts or personal codicils that exceed the well-organized colonial script.[18] Posts+ are not "exit signs" from colonialism, like the way *postracial* or *postcolonial* is sometimes conceived, but sites for reanalyzing colonial and decolonial activities. Apprehending the post+colonial is to feel the beyond and before of it, "the *not yet* and, at times, the *not anymore*" of Indigenous sovereign land and life.[19] In other words, decolonization is the double movement of anticolonialism and rematriation—restoring the futures that Indigenous land and life were meant to follow. This double movement is the fundamental charge of a third world university.

To understand the possibilities for a decolonizing university, we must begin with a discussion of colonialism, particularly the colonizing machine's desires to settle, to self-sustain, to seduce, and to school. This discussion will be informed by my perspective in writing from North America, a settler colonial context, the details of which are not universal. However, even though the analysis is particular to American empire, through it, I unpack the technologies of colonialism that circulate everywhere—particularly the technologies of colonial schooling. More importantly, this analysis urges us to recognize the queer appropriations of these same technologies toward Indigenous and Black and decolonial futures.

As a small book, there are histories and trajectories untold in these pages. I hope you will read this book in relationship to Craig Steven Wilder's *Ebony and Ivy: Race, Slavery, and the Troubled History of America's Universities.* Enslaved people not only labored in and for American universities; their very bodies doubled as the

18. la paperson, "Postcolonial Ghetto."

19. Eve Tuck, "Suspending Damage: A Letter to Communities," *Harvard Educational Review* 79, no. 3 (2009): 417, emphasis original.

literal capital for building and sustaining them—a foundation partially excavated by the 2015 actions of #GU272 at Georgetown University. In *The Imperial University: Academic Repression and Scholarly Dissent,* Piya Chatterjee and Sunaina Maira bring together a collection of voices that detail the imbrication of military and academic complexes, of imperial hegemony and academic repression. Scyborgs practice Black study, strategize and find breath in the undercommons—a fugitive reorganization of the university that Stefano Harney and Fred Moten lyrically describe in *The Undercommons: Fugitive Planning and Black Study.*

This book is further informed by my perspectives as a North American settler "of color," a university professor, and also a community school founder and teacher and organizer within the contradictory apparatuses of public schools and school reform organisms. My position is impossible, a colonialist-by-product of empire, with decolonizing desires. I am, and maybe you are too, a produced colonialist. I am also a by-product of colonization. As a colonialist scrap, I desire against the assemblage that made me.[20] This impossibility motivates this analysis, which seeks not to resolve colonialist dilemmas but to acknowledge that they include specific machined privileges that may be put to work in the service of decolonizations. A recognition of impossibility means to theorize contingently—that is, my thinking is temporary; my right to think aloud is contingent on the apparatus of legitimated colonial knowledge production that ought to be abolished. Theorizing contingently is not to take the ultimate position on what is possible, nor even the penultimate, but rather to commit to analyses that make space for Indigenous sovereign work, to commit to making room for Black and queer thought. This requires refusing to give away too much of what I've overheard or what I think I know. It

---

20. *Colonialist-by-product.* A colonialist (n.) produced by empire. Also, a colonialist (adj.) by-product of empire. I think some readers may relate to this dilemma of being displaced by colonialism, only to arrive at a place as another participant in colonization.

involves limiting the extrapolations of my analyses. I hope to make room for you. May you find some spots in these passages that generate directions for your project. A landing pad, a way station, a taking-off point for your broomstick—that's my goal.

To briefly outline this short book, in chapter 1, I briefly discuss settler colonialism, a framework with which some readers may already feel familiar. For you, I offer the analytic importance of thinking through settler colonial technologies, through those machines that we hate. So although it is a basic outline of settler colonialism, this chapter tries to offer a different tack within theories of settler colonialism to undo some blockages in thinking about blackness, identity, and transnationalism in those theories. I hope this chapter is useful for readers who dislike some of the pitfalls in current theorizations of settler colonialism.

Chapter 2, "Land. And the University Is Settler Colonial," explains how land is a keystone in the modern university through the particular history of land-grant institutions in the United States. I believe this chapter might be a useful synopsis of the significance of land grants and of land as capital.

Chapter 3 asserts that "A Third University Exists within the First." In it, I present the framework that describes the first, second, third, (and fourth) world universities. I offer a diagnosis of the strategic viability for a third world university. I hope you leave this chapter with a sense that decolonizing machines already exist—and that you might be making one of your own.

I end with the scyborg as the agentive element, the decolonizing ghost in the colonizing machine. Throughout this discussion, I use historic examples of scyborgs but treat them as historically present; that is, the "active sense of presence," to borrow a phrase from Gerald Vizenor, of the decolonial spirit that began with the colonial university's inception is already present today.[21] Scyborg

21. Gerald Robert Vizenor, "Resistance in the Blood," in *Youth Resistance Research and Theories of Change,* ed. Eve Tuck and K. Wayne Yang (New York: Routledge, 2014), 114.

traces are present throughout the machinery. Pieces of other scyborgs may be present inside your own circuitry, and yours in others. Those pieces may lend to your flight, may bend to your will for a bit, and may have a collective, transhistorical will of their own. Scyborg is shorthand for structural agency. The scyborg operates within and without apparatuses. S-he is the decolonial rider within the circuitry of colonizing machines, and hir black gown is continuous with the carbon dust that smokes through their best hermetically sealed works. The scyborg moves at multiple scales; the scyborg is personal; the scyborg is collective. The difference between the scyborg and other orgs in the machine is that the scyborg grasps hir decolonial possibilities. S-he knows hir broomstick can't carry hir beyond colonization, but with it, s-he might rake together a decolonizing golem. Maybe you could be scyborg, and so I'm writing to maybe you. If so, cite me not, and ghost-ride this book.

Settler Colonialism Is a Set of Technologies

> I learned that our land was not quite our land; that our compound was part of property owned by an African landlord . . . that we were now *ahoi*, tenants at will. How did we come to be *ahoi* on our own land?
>
> —NGŨGĨ WA Thiong'o, *Dreams in a Time of War*

IN *DREAMS IN A TIME OF WAR*, the first book in a trilogy of memoirs, Ngũgĩ wa Thiong'o begins with land. The dispossession of Indigenous Kenyans from their land, his Gĩkũyũ family's dispossession from their traditional lands in particular, was made legally possible through the legitimation of the printed English word over the millennia-old word of the Gĩkũyũ people. How land becomes property not only was but is still the great colonizing trick that paves the way for capitalist accumulation.

Indigenous land rights in Kenya were and are still largely guided by customary law, which evolved over millennia to describe clan and community rights to cultivation, freedom of use, and stewardship of land. Under customary law, land often cannot be permanently alienated into property. Nineteenth-century British colonial authorities found it convenient to respect customary law, as it seemed to preclude African land titles, and colonialists actually used customary law to justify the forced labor of Indigenous Africans as "cultivators." However, Kenya's "white highlands" of the Gĩkũyũ became one of the few hotbeds of white settlement outside of South Africa. There, lands of Indigenous Africans were declared terra nullius, making way for white land titles, and as the land was bought and sold under their homes and under their feet, the Gĩkũyũ became tenants on their own land. When needed to be removed, they became designated as "squatters." In 1948, British colonialists extended the Indian Act to Kenya, a legal claim to convert (Black) Indigenous land into British Crown lands and Black (Indigenous) peoples into Crown subjects.[1] In this example, we can see the separations of Black–Indigenous, people–land, and the simultaneous extension of white sovereignty over these now separate lands and peoples. Technologies of alienation, separation, conversion of land into property and of people into targets of subjection, continue to mutate. Black bodies become squatters, become subjects of the Crown, then of the colonial state, and now of the state of Kenya. Settlers become protected by rule of force; their violence against Black "squatters" becomes legitimate; state violence becomes normalized repertoire. Black bodies become exchangeable juridical objects to be recast as needed for settler property making. Settler colonialism is about the land. Yet, technologies to make land into property also remake Indigenous African bodies.

Land is the prime concern of settler colonialism, contexts in which the colonizer comes to a "new" place not only to seize and exploit but to stay, making that "new" place his permanent home. Settler colonialism thus complicates the center–periphery model that was classically used to describe colonialism, wherein an imperial center, the "metropole," dominates distant colonies, the "periphery." Typically, one thinks of European colonization of Africa, India, the Caribbean, the Pacific Islands, in terms of exter-

1. Reem Gafar, "Women's Land and Property Rights in Kenya," Center for Women's Land Rights, October 14, 2014, http://landwise.resourceequity .org/guides/8/generate_pdf#customary-land-tenure-in-formal-law; Valentine Wakoko, "The Evolution of Land Law in Kenya," https://www .academia.edu/8972722/THE_EVOLUTION_OF_LAND_LAW_IN_KENYA; Dietmar Rothermund, *The Routledge Companion to Decolonization,* Routledge Companions to History (New York: Routledge, 2006).

nal colonialism, also called exploitation colonialism, where land and human beings are recast as natural resources for primitive accumulation: coltan, petroleum, diamonds, water, salt, seeds, genetic material, chattel. Theories named as "settler colonial studies" had a resurgence beginning around 2006.[2] However, the analysis of settler colonialism is actually not new, only often ignored within Western critiques of empire.[3] The critical literatures of the colonized have long positioned the violence of settlement as a prime feature in colonial life as well as in global arrangements of power. We can see this in Franz Fanon's foundational critiques of colonialism. Whereas Fanon's work is often generalized for its diagnoses of anti/colonial violence and the racialized psychoses of colonization upon colonized and colonizer, Fanon is also talking about settlement as the particular feature of French colonization in Algeria. For Fanon, the violence of French colonization in Algeria arises from settlement as a spatial immediacy of empire: the geospatial collapse of metropole and colony into the same time and place. On the "selfsame land" are spatialized white immunity and racialized violation, non-Native desires for freedom, Black life, and Indigenous relations.[4]

2. This resurgence in academic circles can be marked by the luminary work of Patrick Wolfe, "Settler Colonialism and the Elimination of the Native," *Journal of Genocide Research* 8, no. 4 (2006): 387–409, and Lorenzo Verancini, *Israel and Settler Society* (London: Pluto Books, 2006), and with the founding of the journal *Settler Colonial Studies* in 2011. While acknowledging the importance of the resurgence, I do not want to narrate critical theorizations of settler colonialism as somehow originating from this moment.

3. E.g., Michael Hardt and Antonio Negri, *Empire* (Cambridge, Mass.: Harvard University Press, 2000).

4. Frantz Fanon, *The Wretched of the Earth* (New York: Grove Press, 1963); Albert Memmi, *The Colonizer and the Colonized,* BP 232 (Boston: Beacon Press, 1967); Eve Tuck, Allison Guess, and Hannah Sultan, "Not Nowhere: Collaborating on Selfsame Land," *Decolonization: Indigeneity, Education, and Society,* June 26, 2014, https://decolonization.files.wordpress .com/2014/06/notnowhere-pdf.pdf.

Settler colonialism is too often thought of as "what happened" to Indigenous people. This kind of thinking confines the experiences of Indigenous people, their critiques of settler colonialism, their decolonial imaginations, to an unwarranted historicizing parochialism, as if settler colonialism were a past event that "happened to" Native peoples and not generalizable to non-Natives. Actually, settler colonialism is something that "happened for" settlers. Indeed, it is happening for them/us right now. Wa Thiong'o's question of how instead of why directs us to think of land tenancy laws, debt, and the privatization of land as settler colonial technologies that enable the "eventful" history of plunder and disappearance. Property law is a settler colonial technology. The weapons that enforce it, the knowledge institutions that legitimize it, the financial institutions that operationalize it, are also technologies. Like all technologies, they evolve and spread.

Recasting land as property means severing Indigenous peoples from land. This separation, what Hortense Spillers describes as "the loss of Indigenous name/land" for Africans-turned-chattel, recasts Black Indigenous people as black bodies for biopolitical disposal: who will be moved where, who will be murdered how, who will be machinery for what, and who will be made property for whom.[5] In the alienation of land from life, alienable rights are produced: the right to own (property), the right to law (protection through legitimated violence), the right to govern (supremacist sovereignty), the right to have rights (humanity). In a word, what is produced is whiteness. Moreover, it is not just human beings who are refigured in the schism. Land and nonhumans become alienable properties, a move that first alienates land from its own sovereign life. Thus we can speak of the various technologies required to create and maintain these separations, these alienations: Black from Indigenous, human from nonhuman, land from life.[6]

5. Hortense J. Spillers, "Mama's Baby, Papa's Maybe: An American Grammar Book," *Diacritics* 17, no. 2 (1987): 73.

6. In this book, *Black* refers to Black life, people, epistemologies,

"How?" is a question you ask if you are concerned with the mechanisms, not just the motives, of colonization. Instead of settler colonialism as an ideology, or as a history, you might consider settler colonialism as a set of technologies—a frame that could help you to forecast colonial next operations and to plot decolonial directions.

This chapter proceeds with the following insights. (1) The settler–native–slave triad does not describe identities. The triad—an analytic mainstay of settler colonial studies—digs a pitfall of identity that not only chills collaborations but also implies that the racial will be the solution. (2) Technologies are trafficked. Technologies generate patterns of social relations to land. Technologies mutate, and so do these relationships. Colonial technologies travel. In tracing technologies' past and future trajectories, we can connect how settler colonial and antiblack technologies circulate in transnational arenas. (3) Land—not just people—is the biopolitical target.[7] The examples are many: fracking, biopiracy, damming of rivers and flooding of valleys, the carcasses of pigs that die from the feed additive ractopamine and are allowable for harvest by the U.S. Food and Drug Administration. The subjugation of land and nonhuman life to deathlike states *in order to* support "human" life is a "biopolitics" well beyond the Foucauldian conception of biopolitical as governmentality or the neoliberal disciplining of modern, bourgeois, "human" subject. (4) (Y)our task is to theorize in the break, that is, to refuse the master

---

and the Black radical tradition, whereas *black* refers to the distortion of blackness into the role of referent for a racial order under white supremacist logics; black is a category of antiblackness, whereas Black was always beyond whiteness and antiblackness—as Fred Moten puts it, "beyond dispossession."

7. *Land* is shorthand for land, waters, air, plant and animal life, and Indigenous peoples—in other words, Indigenous worlds in their specific contexts. *Land/life* is shorthand I use to emphasize that land/life are in relation within Indigenous cosmologies but are actively being separated by colonizing operations.

narrative that technology is loyal to the master, that (y)our theory has a Eurocentric origin. Black studies, Indigenous studies, and Other-ed studies have already made their breaks with Foucault (over biopolitics), with Deleuze and Guatarri (over assemblages and machines), and with Marx (over life and primitive accumulation). (5) Even when they are dangerous, understanding technologies provides us some pathways for decolonizing work. We can identify projects of collaboration on decolonial technologies. Colonizing mechanisms are evolving into new forms, and they might be subverted toward decolonizing operations.

The Settler–Native–Slave Triad Does Not Describe Identities

One of the main interventions of settler colonial studies has been to insist that the patterning of social relations is shaped by colonialism's thirst for land and thus is shaped to fit modes of empire. Because colonialism is a perverted affair, our relationships are also warped into complicitous arrangements of violation, trespass, and collusion with its mechanisms.

For Fanon, the psychosis of colonialism arises from the patterning of violence into the binary relationship between the immune humanity of the white settler and the impugned humanity of the native. For Fanon, the supremacist "right" to create settler space that is immune from violence, and the "right" to abuse the body of the Native to maintain white immunity, this is the spatial and fleshy immediacy of settler colonialism. Furthermore, the "humanity" of the settler is constructed upon his agency over the land and nature. As Maldonado-Torres explains, "I think, therefore I am" is actually an articulation of "I conquer, therefore I am," a sense of identity posited upon the harnessing of nature and its "natural" people.[8] This creates a host of post+colonial problems

8. Nelson Maldonado-Torres, "On the Coloniality of Being: Contributions to the Development of a Concept," *Cultural Studies* 21, no. 2–3 (2007): 240–70.

that have come to define modernity. Because the humanity of the settler is predicated on his ability to "write the world," to make history upon and over the natural world, the colonized is instructed to make her claim to humanity by similarly acting on the world or, more precisely, acting in his. Indeed, for Fanon, it is the perverse ontology of settler becomings—becoming landowner or becoming property, becoming killable or becoming a killer—and the mutual implication of tortured and torturer that mark the psychosis of colonialism.

This problem of modernity and colonial psychosis is echoed in Jack Forbes's writings:

> Columbus was a wétiko. He was mentally ill or insane, the carrier of a terribly contagious psychological disease, the wétiko psychosis. . . .
>   The wétiko psychosis, and the problems it creates, have inspired many resistance movements and efforts at reform or revolution. Unfortunately, most of these efforts have failed because they have never diagnosed the wétiko.[9]

Under Western modernity, becoming "free" means becoming a colonizer, and because of this, "the central contradiction of modernity is freedom."[10]

Critiques of settler colonialism, therefore, do not offer just another "type" of colonialism to add to the literature but a mode of analysis that has repercussions for any diagnosis of coloniality and for understanding the modern conditions of freedom. By *modern conditions* of freedom, I mean that Western freedom is a product of colonial modernity, and I mean that such freedom comes with conditions, with strings attached, most manifest as terms of unfreedom for nonhumans. As Cindi Mayweather says, "your freedom's in a bind."[11]

9. Jack D. Forbes, *Columbus and Other Cannibals: The Wétiko Disease of Exploitation, Imperialism, and Terrorism*, rev. ed. (New York: Seven Stories Press, 2008), 22–172.

10. Ruth Wilson Gilmore, afterword to Tuck and Yang, *Youth Resistance Research and Theories of Change,* 230.

11. "Janelle Monae—Many Moons [Official Short Film]," YouTube

For grasping the twisted plotlines written by colonialism, the *settler–native–slave triad* is one of the most useful and most problematic heuristics in settler colonial studies. This triad is useful because it quickly describes the crooked relationships constructed by settler colonialism: the settler who accumulates rights, land, and property; the native whose presence on land must be extinguished; the chattel slave who must be kept landless. Although simple, it nonetheless quickly complicates the binaries in terms of which we are trained to think: oppressor–oppressed, black–white, settler–native. Even though white supremacy might be a prime architect in the triad, a triadic analysis decenters white supremacy as the absolute pole or umbrella of oppression. Instead, it shows our skewed participation in the colonization of other peoples and places. We are all complicit, just some of us a lot more than others. We can think of the triad as a quick sketch of colonialism on a napkin. It is useful for drawing attention to a complicated problem and for disrupting other paradigms. That is about how useful it is.

However, the settler–native–slave triad has also forwarded many problems, in large part because it seems to describe racial identities: settlers, Indigenous peoples, and Black people. Thinking of this triad as identities creates major pitfalls—four of which are pointed out in what follows. The most obvious is the misconstrued question, are Black people settlers? This question is symptomatic of a pitfall of settler elision, where everyone non-Native is assumed to fit the category of settler: settlers = non-Natives = people of color = migrants of color = settlers of color = Black people. Such a question cannot reckon with how Black people are often confronted by the *impossibility* of settlement, because antiblackness positions Black people as "out of place" on land. More revealing questions would be more specific: when and where have Black communities been settlers? When and where do they cease to be

---

video, posted by janellemonae, October 3, 2008, https://www.youtube.com/watch?v=LHgbzNHVg0c.

settlers? The same might be asked of other communities, Black and not, indeed, Indigenous and not. Such questions are not directly engaged by the triad, because "the slave" is not shorthand for a generalizable anywhere, anytime Black community anyway.

We have another pitfall of turning the triad into an identity spectrum, where settler–native–slave are thought of as points on a graph and individuals or ethnic groups can be located partway between different categories. Settler–native–slave technologies operate everywhere on everybody in intersecting, sometimes contradictory ways, and always with a dynamic specificity that radically changes with context. Antiblack technologies operate on Mien people in Oakland, California, in 2016 differently from how antiblack/anti-Indigenous/pro-settler technologies might try to reconstruct Mien students into Asian students just a few miles away at UC Berkeley.

We have the pitfall of anthropocentricism. Anthropocentric analyses of colonialism prefer to talk about colonized peoples, not animals, earth, water, and air. This continual return to the racialized human subject—which is identity's main referent—undermines the work that Indigenous studies has done to emphasize the geopolitical, the land, and the circle of relations that do not begin and end with the human.

Finally, we have another pitfall of untranslatability of North American identities to non-North settings, because settler–native–slave do not map neatly onto other racialized groups elsewhere.

If not identities, then what are the settler–native–slave in the triad? The triad is a figurative shorthand—settler–native–slave are figurae to describe relations of power with respect to land. They sound like identities, but they are not identities per se. As figurae, they represent sites of exception that reveal the underlying logic of settler colonial power. As a suitable analogy, sites of exception are like planets, supernovae, and black holes. None is quite comparable to the others; yet each can be analyzed for its particular gravitational effects, which in interaction come to define the field of gravity in the surrounding space. Sites of exception are not comparable, even though their effects can be felt as an interlocking lattice of power. The "settler" is a juridical space; the "native" is a world to be disavowed and dismembered; the "slave" is an ontological system. Space, world, and system are not of the same scale or form. They are not comparable units of analysis.

The "settler" is not an identity; it is the idealized juridical space of exceptional rights granted to normative settler citizens and the idealized exceptionalism by which the settler state exerts its sovereignty. The "settler" is a site of exception from which whiteness emerges. Whiteness is property; it is the right to have rights; it is the legal human; the anthropocentric normal is written in its image. Not all settlers at all times enjoy the full privileges available to the "settler"; rather, settler supremacy is constructed and maintained by a number of technologies: citizenship, private property, civil and criminal innocence, normative settler sexuality, and so on. Settler technologies may be to your advantage always, sometimes, or never, depending on who you are, where you are, and what time it is.[12]

The "native" is not an Indigenous identity; it is a world to be obliterated, exceptionalized as the necropolitical target, and also to be splintered into pieces that are constructed as "naturally" eligible for "primitive accumulation."[13] The "native" is a site of exception for that which and those who are written as premodern, primitive, and thus "before" law and "before" rights. The "native" is thus exceptionalized from having any recognizable laws or rights that matter

12. This sentence is not meant to make settlers feel better—to flatten "oppression" into a relativism. Even if it isn't always to their advantage, individual settlers tend to uphold settler supremacy because of its relative advantage (over immigrants yet-to-become settlers) and its promise of unending advantage over Black people, Indigenous people.

13. Imperial accumulation under Marxist rubric is usually considered "primitive accumulation," or "previous accumulation," which is an antecedent to capitalist accumulation. Yet, for colonized lands and peoples, there is nothing "previous" or somehow over about imperial accumulation—it is modern, continuing, evolving.

in modernity. Technologies of Indigenous erasure include military materiel and methodologies to carry out terror or genocide or containment; frontier law that legitimates murder, rape, torture, and abduction; racial science of disappearance (such as blood quantum); the partitioning of earth into "natural resources" that can be separated, owned, sold, and developed; land privation, privatization, fungibility, and development; boarding schools and institutions of cultural assimilation; resource development and cultivation, and so on. Technologies of Indigenous erasure are applied to Indigenous people, but some are also applied to enemy Others in war, some are recommissioned to reinvent spaces of frontier and border, some are used to gentrify and redevelop ghettoized space.[14] Anti-indigenous technologies are applied to nonhumans—sometimes specifically to eliminate Indigenous people, such as killing the buffalo as a means to starve Plains peoples; sometimes in the name of progress, such as the killing of Haitian Kreyòl pigs; sometimes as a reflex of desecration, such as the poisoning of nonwhite waters. Primitive accumulation involves not only the gathering of "natural" resources as assets but also the externalizing of the "cost" of the accumulation in the form of contaminated water, disease, and other traumas to the "natural," nonpropertied, that is, "indigenous," world. To be subject to anti-Indian technologies does not require you to be an Indigenous person.

The "slave" describes how blackness is transfigured into enslavability and murderability. The "slave" should not be analyzed as a category of labor that "reduces Blackness to a mere tool of settlement" but rather as an ontology of total fungibility and unending property constitutive of the very world order of settler colonialism.[15] That is, the logic of racial capital creates an indefinite

14. la paperson, "A Ghetto Land Pedagogy: An Antidote for Settler Environmentalism," *Environmental Education Research* 20, no. 1 (2014): 115–30; Angie Morrill, "Time Traveling Dogs (and Other Native Feminist Ways to Defy Dislocations)," *Cultural Studies↔Critical Methodologies* 17, no. 1 (2017).

15. Tiffany King, "Labor's Aphasia: Toward Antiblackness as Constitutive to Settler Colonialism," *Decolonization: Indigeneity, Education,*

being of property to be exchanged, to be shipped or stored, to be parted out, to be disposed. The technologies of antiblackness create ontological illegality or criminal presence, landlessness, lethal geographies, carceral apparatuses, trafficking and abduction, nonpersonhood, and so on. Obviously, technologies of antiblackness circulate onto non-Black bodies. In a U.S.–Mexican borderland context, for example, we see the condensation of antiblack and anti-Indigenous technologies to dispose of brown bodies and to create frontier space—a militarized zone of policing and death. In North American ghetto contexts, we see the wide-scale application of antiblack technologies upon whole communities who can be of mixed ethnicities. However, one incomparable technology of antiblackness is the production of the Black body as in itself the preeminent site for antiblackness.[16] Whereas settler technologies can focus on space, and technologies of Indigenous erasure can focus on land, technologies of antiblackness have a corporeal priority.

Technologies Are Trafficked

Thinking about technologies moves us a little bit out of the trap of thinking about specific identities as well-defined colonizers or as the fixed targets of necropolitics. Instead, we can see the transit of empire as involving a commute of technologies and a translation of ideologies and logics[17]—a moving cross hair.

and Society, June 10, 2014; see also Frank B. Wilderson, Red, White, and Black: Cinema and the Structure of U.S. Antagonisms (Durham, N.C.: Duke University Press, 2010); Tiffany Jeannette King, "In the Clearing: Black Female Bodies, Space, and Settler Colonial Landscapes," PhD diss., University of Maryland, 2013.

16. Alexander G. Weheliye, Habeas Viscus: Racializing Assemblages, Biopolitics, and Black Feminist Theories of the Human (Durham, N.C.: Duke University Press, 2014).

17. Steven Salaita and Peter Gran, The Holy Land in Transit: Colonialism and the Quest for Canaan (Syracuse, N.Y.: Syracuse University Press, 2006); Jodi A. Byrd, The Transit of Empire: Indigenous Critiques of Colonialism (Minneapolis: University of Minnesota Press, 2011).

This is also why we can analyze the technologies of whiteness, antiblackness, and Indigenous erasure in contexts where there is no apparent white colonizer or phenotypically black person, or ostensibly where "everyone is indigenous" to a country. Technologies of land dispossession are in wide circulation today even in places where we do not see white settler emplacement. For example, the privatization of land in China employs settler colonial technologies, creating indebted dispossessed people by erasing any pre-state land rights. Indeed, Mao Zedong claimed that Indigenous peoples' rights were irrelevant in China, because the revolution resolved all such dilemmas. In China as well as in Mexico, revolutionary nationalisms claim innocence from colonial processes by claiming a "new future starting now"—conveniently ignoring that its revolution is predicated upon nation-state technology. In Mexico, the concept of *mestizaje* was transfigured by Mexican neocolonial statecraft into a universal transcendental race, by such luminary statebuilders as José Vasconcelos.[18] In such cases, the settler nation appropriates indigeneity to manufacture a national "ethnicity" that serves dual ends of Indigenous appropriation domestically and a way of exporting a distinct, national "tradition" abroad. Stating that "all of us" Mexican nationals are *Indigena en parte* is another way of saying that your Indigeneity is not special, that *none of you* are truly Indigenous anymore. In South Korea, where ostensibly all Koreans are "indigenous" to the peninsula, we witness Indigenous displacement in the logic of neoliberal expansion: the people are increasingly removed from their ancestral homelands and plugged in to the growing South Korean transnational corporate machinery.

18. Vasconcelos served as Mexico's minister of education immediately after the Mexican Revolution in 1914 and then as the founding secretary of education in 1920. José Vasconcelos, *La Raza Cósmica: Misión de La Raza Iberoamericana: Notas de Viajes a La América de Sur* (Paris: Agencia mundial de librería, 1925).

With "machinery," I am drawing from Eve Tuck's reading (and eventual refusal) of Foucault's and Deleuze and Guattari's theorizations of "desiring machines": assemblages of machines that attach to, accumulate, and create other machines.[19] The settler desires to become the native. His machines turn the Native into chattel and/or subtracts her indigeneity to make her less and less native.[20] Machines of genocide, enslavement, land mining, and war run through the colonial apparatus and produce multiple colonialisms as adaptations to each particular place and time. This is why specific colonial apparatuses differ but similar technologies recirculate in them—pieces of desiring machines that assemble into new machines.

Thus a technological rather than identity–political analysis of the settler–native–slave triad allows us to see the "how" and the "who next" rather than just the "who" of settler colonialism. The triad is a structure of settler colonialism. The relationships it maps were never the ones we loved in the first place. It describes what power wants, not who you are.

Land Is the Biopolitical Target

Biopolitics is normally conceptualized in terms of how "life" for the modern human subject is increasingly controlled by liberal disciplinary apparatuses. Yet the exercises of supremacist sovereign power over life and death are most chillingly undisguised when we consider the ways the life worlds of land, air, water, plants and animals, and Indigenous peoples are reconfigured into natural resources, chattel, and waste: statuses whose capitalist

19. Eve Tuck, "Breaking Up with Deleuze: Desire and Valuing the Irreconcilable," *International Journal of Qualitative Studies in Education* 23, no. 5 (2010): 635–50.

20. I this book, I capitalize *Native* and *Indigenous* to refer to identities, cultures, and epistemologies of Indigenous nations, communities, and tribal groups. I use lowercase *native* and *indigenous* when explicitly referring to settler and Western concepts of native and indigenous.

"value" does not depend on whether they are living or dead but only on their fungibility and disposability. For example, in modern animal industrial processes, the carcass is valued just as much as, if not more than, the breathing animal. The business of chicken "farming" involves the separation of birds into parts with exchangeable value, extractable value, or disposable value: skinless, boneless white meat offers premium profit per ounce; parts not fitting an American appetite are frozen and dumped with undercutting prices in poorer countries; viscera go to rendering plants to become pet food or fertilizer; feathers return as animal feed or plastic fortifiers; beaks are routinely pared off of live birds to prevent damage before slaughter. Fungibility is exchangeability. Fungibility also means getting anatomized into exchangeable parts to be stored, shipped, sold, combined with other parts for a new product, or decomposed entirely for elimination. When parts are worth more than the whole, the living being ceases to exist as a meaningful unit. Fungibility means that "life" is reduced to just another state of matter, to plug and play into machines of re/production. Chickens grow like vines into cages; cattle are planted in boxes of mud where they are watered, fertilized, and fed growth serum. In modern animal industrial processes, the "livestock" are already in a state of living death.

In discussing the state of ambiguous life/death, I am directly drawing upon Black studies scholarship in the vein of Wynter and Weheliye, who describe how antiblackness situates the Black body outside of any meaningful speciation with the human.[21] Hortense Spillers describes how slave transactions were recorded with a meticulous disregard for gender and name—just like counting livestock: "nothing breaks the uniformity of this guise," this "sameness of anonymous portrayal," despite the otherwise "detail and precision that characterize these accounts."[22] In contrast to

21. Katherine McKittrick, *Sylvia Wynter: On Being Human as Praxis* (Durham, N.C.: Duke University Press, 2014); Weheliye, *Habeas Viscus.*

22. Hortense J. Spillers, *Black, White, and in Color: Essays on American*

the rubric of Marxist politics that focuses on the labor exploitation faced by human slaughterhouse workers, Afropessimist scholar Frank Wilderson compares the accumulation of Black bodies with the cows in the slaughterhouse. "But still we must ask, what about the cows? The cows are not being exploited, they are being accumulated and, if need be, killed."[23] Writing on neoslavery and the modern prison's genealogy in the techniques of the transatlantic slave trade, Dennis Childs describes the literal and figurative caging of Black ontology into a state of "living death."[24] Antiblack is not a subject position. It is a chattel position—like being a sardine in a can—a Schrödinger's box where life and death are only two different states of a commodity.

Tiffany Lethabo King takes this analysis a step further by considering how the body of the Black woman is treated much as land is treated under slavery and settler colonialism. That is, the settler colonial machinery that marks up land for clearing, for production, for settlement, for industry, for waste—for infinite malleability in the service of settler futures—similarly marks the Black woman as infinitely malleable in the service of a racial economy. "Black-femaleness becomes this open sign within the symbolic economy of slavery. It can be turned into virtually anything": productive labor, reproductive labor, tissue for medical science, object of social policy, and "anything else imaginable." Anything, that is, except human. For King, Black women's bodies function as metaphors for and units of settler space:

> It is within Black feminist scholarship that we see this robust theorization of Black fungibility or the unending exchangeability. . . . To gender Blackness as "female" is to make Blackness more malleable and flexible as opposed to making it, as Sylvia Wynter says, "another

---

Literature and Culture (Chicago: University of Chicago Press, 2003), 216.

23. Frank Wilderson III, "Gramsci's Black Marx: Whither the Slave in Civil Society?," *Social Identities* 9, no. 2 (2003): 233.

24. Dennis Childs, *Slaves of the State* (Minneapolis: University of Minnesota Press, 2015).

genre of" the liberal stable human (i.e., white womanhood). What this means, is that gender as a discourse when applied to Black bodies is about making these bodies ever malleable. It is not about imposing coherent humanizing gender upon Black Bodies.[25]

King's analysis thus extends our understanding of Black fungibility beyond the animal and into land, into the nonhuman beyond biological. In this way, King's insights have provocations for the very relationship between the fields of Indigenous studies and Black studies. Whereas Blackness is obscured in ethnic studies as another "race," it has greater capaciousness when thought about as a piece of the more-than-human world—the living world—as analyzed more deeply in Indigenous studies.

When foundational Native studies scholar Jack Forbes asks, "where do our bodies end?" he draws attention to life as being far more than the unit of the living organism:

I can lose my hands, and still live. I can lose my legs and still live. I can lose my eyes and still live. I can lose my hair, eyebrows, nose, arms, and many other things and still live. But if I lose the air I die. If I lose the sun I die. If I lose the earth I die. If I lose the water I die. If I lose the plants and animals I die. All of these things are more a part of me, more essential to my every breath, than is my so-called body. What is my real body?

We are not autonomous, self-sufficient beings as European mythology teaches. . . . We are rooted just like the trees. But our roots come out of our nose and mouth, like an umbilical cord, forever connected to the rest of the world. . . . Nothing that we do, do we do by ourselves. We do not see by ourselves. We do not hear by ourselves. . . . That which the tree exhales, I inhale. That which I exhale, the trees inhale. Together we form a circle.[26]

When we consider the transport of fracked oil via railways and pipelines, and the bulldozing of the Standing Rock Sioux tribe's burial sites by the forces of Dakota Access Pipeline, we see the

25. Tiffany Lethabo King, "Interview with Tiffany Lethabo King," *Feral Feminisms*, no. 4 (2015): 65.

26. Forbes, *Columbus and Other Cannibals*, 145–46.

application of death to land itself. Destroying burial sites to lay pipeline is no different from the mass extermination of buffalo to lay rail. Both target the land (the nonhuman) to (1) eliminate Indigenous presence and (2) make the land alienable. Making death lands is an operation of making terra nullius. Death and extraction and fungibility ride together.

Alienating the life out of Black life is required to subject black bodies to industrial technologies of mass killing and caging. Alienating the Indigenous spirit life out of the land is required to subject land/animals/people to mass reapings. Removing land from people also means making war ontologically inherent on certain peoples. War-able peoples in turn lead to bombable lands, extinctionable animals, and genocide. The "human" is about all the idealizations above the flesh and above the land, what Sylvia Wynter describes as the elevation of an "ethnoclass" of the Western bourgeois conception of Man, "which overrepresents itself as if it were the human itself."[27] Blackness is about the flesh, and the flesh is land—both are biomatter. Thus, by seeing land as biopolitical, I am seeing how the nonhuman critique in Black studies aligns with the more-than-human critique in Indigenous studies.

Settler time has transfigured North American land into a simultaneity of Black violation and Indigenous disappearance, into a schism of property–people. Therefore, for King, the entanglements of settler colonialism and gendered/sexualized antiblackness must inform solidarity in Native and Black feminist organizing. Land must be decolonized into a simultaneity of Black life as *being,* which requires Black places to *be,* and to be joyful, without the eminent threat of violation and of Indigenous life as *being-and-place,* which requires places/peoples to be regenerated. This is a decolonizing land biopolitics, so to speak.

27. Sylvia Wynter, "Unsettling the Coloniality of Being/Power/Truth/Freedom: Towards the Human, after Man, Its Overrepresentation—an Argument," *CR: The New Centennial Review* 3, no. 3 (2004): 260.

Theorize in the Break

For the reader who is concerned with the genealogy of theory, especially for you who will shape this theory into your own, know that by deploying the "biopolitical" and "technologies," you do not have to allow yourself to be claimed into a Eurocentric lineage. Rather, the genealogy of (y)our theory lies in the breaks as theorized by Black and Indigenous intellectuals.

The object—which is not a human subject, which is the state of Black being that is already outside of the "human" ethnoclass of Man—resists, according to Fred Moten. The object resists Eurocentric theory "by way of open analytic failure" of that theory; in other words, it resists by dwelling in the "breakdown of the breakdown." To theorize in the break is to theorize in an elsewhere that is already beyond the dispossession of that oppressive theory, "by way of a kind of recapitulative improvisation (a lingering in the iconic break of this double breakdown)."[28] Put plainly, to theorize in the break is to improvise theory in the rupture from the genealogy of the (often European) founding fathers. It is to think, sing, write, and embody theory in the elsewhere, in the sovereign, in the Black.

By theorizing machinery, you do not have to embrace Gilles Deleuze, despite the totalizing sweep of his and Félix Guattari's thinking. In "Breaking up with Deleuze," Eve Tuck parses out differences between her understandings of knowledge, change, and regeneration and those pieces of Deleuzian theory of desire that seem to echo Indigenous understanding. Unlike the unconscious directions of Deleuzian desiring machines, Tuck "insists that desire accrues wisdom in assemblage, and does so over generations."[29] Eve Tuck broke up with Deleuze so that you may avoid his seductions.

---

28. Fred Moten, *In the Break: The Aesthetics of the Black Radical Tradition* (Minneapolis: University of Minnesota Press, 2003), 140.
29. Tuck, "Breaking Up with Deleuze," 644.

Likewise, theorizing land as biopolitical target is better understood through Achille Mbembe's necropolitics than through Michel Foucault's biopolitics. Mbembe breaks from Foucault's interest in the disciplining of liberal life by examining the "subjugation of life to the power of death."[30] One can see how necropower has long been in effect in settler colonial invasions of Indigenous lands—and has evolved its killing, capturing, and living-dead zombie technologies.[31]

Black studies has already made multiple breaks with the Western project of uplifting and theorizing "humanity." In theorizing the human, or the genealogy of prisons, or capitalism, or gender, or justice, Black studies scholarship continues to denude how antiblackness is the normalized exception upon which Western politics, theories, and institutions are erected.[32] For example, Alexander Weheliye deconstructs the analytic failures of Eurocentric biopolitical theory—the breakdown of the breakdown—particularly how Giorgio Agamben's bare life and Foucault's biopolitical racism assume pained flesh to be an exercise of exceptional power. Following Saidiya Hartman, Weheliye demonstrates the regularity of the brutalization of (black) flesh under colonialism and slavery.[33]

Finally, land as biopolitical also draws upon global studies of biopiracy and of neoliberalism. Kalindi Vora breaks with Marx to insightfully describe how Global South human organs, time,

30. Achille Mbembe, "Necropolitics," *Public Culture* 15, no. 1 (2003): 39.

31. I use *biopolitics* instead of *necropolitics* in this writing because *bio-* hails a living and dying world beyond the human, whereas *necro-* is usually reserved for human death. But there is no difference between biopolitics and necropolitics made in this book (I know they are different).

32. McKittrick, *Sylvia Wynter*; Childs, *Slaves of the State*; Cedric J. Robinson, *Black Marxism: The Making of the Black Radical Tradition* (Chapel Hill: University of North Carolina Press, 1983); Spillers, *Black, White, and in Color*; Saidiya V. Hartman, *Scenes of Subjection: Terror, Slavery, and Self-Making in Nineteenth-Century America* (Oxford: Oxford University Press, 1997).

33. Weheliye, *Habeas Viscus*; Hartman, *Scenes of Subjection*.

intelligence, social life, and biological life functions are tapped to support cosmopolitan "life" in the Global North. "Vital energies" are drained and redirected to perform liberal "life support."[34] This moves away from the anthropocentric sense of "biopolitical" as principally referring to the control of life/death for human populations, when the very methods of life/death involve the bleeding of Indigenous worlds to pump life into a "First World."

In each of these breaks, there is always a defender of European intellectual hegemony who wishes to claim blackness back in service of that which wishes itself white: Reviewers of Mbembe's work who say necropolitics is no different from biopolitics; reviewers of Vora's work who says life support is the same as capitalist labor exploitation; the Marxists who would claim, once again, that Marx predicted it all.

Here, in the breaks, are possible dovetails among Black, Indigenous, and Other-ed studies that make the foundation for a technologies framework. Technologies are the master's tools, and yet they will never be just that, any more than you are the master's tool. Your theory is just like that.

Even When They Are Dangerous

Everywhere land resists and refuses—whales that destroy ships, bees that refuse to work, bombed islands that reconstitute themselves. The land also resists in the form of people; Indigenous peoples' resistance is the land's resistance. Indigenous people continue to subvert legal and capitalist technologies as part of that resistance. And technologies and technological beings resist too.

Patent law is patently designed to favor corporations, a legal technology whose colonizing functions are particularly evident when considering how Monsanto and other GMO producing gi-

---

34. Kalindi Vora, *Life Support: Biocapital and the New History of Outsourced Labor*, Difference Incorporated (Minneapolis: University of Minnesota Press, 2015).

ants are patenting seeds and genes they "find" throughout the world. Yet Indigenous communities are fighting this biopiracy by refusing the systems that permit corporations to patent life and that document knowledge for expropriation in the first place, by creating digital libraries of traditional knowledges, and sometimes by subverting patent law to claim rights to their own life worlds and knowledges.[35]

Treaties are technologies of colonial coercion and yet also of Indigenous survivance. As Scott Lyon says, an x-mark that signs the treaty "is a sign of consent in a context of coercion. . . . And yet there is always the possibility of slippage, indeterminacy, unforeseen consequences, or unintended results; it is always possible, that is, that an x-mark could result in something good. Why else, we must ask, would someone bother to make it?"[36] Since 1948, the Oneida Indian Nation has pursued restoration of sovereignty over historical reservation lands via a complex set of avenues involving treaty law, U.S. courts, casinos, and excise taxes, resulting in a landmark 13,004 acres of land taken into trust by the Department of the Interior in 2014.[37]

Sometimes settlers return land to Indigenous tribes and nations. Hopefully, they/we might do so without conditions. As I write, the Kashia Band of Pomo Indians are getting back 688 acres of coastal

35. Mohan Dewan, "The Realities of Traditional Knowledge and Patents in India," Intellectual Property Watch, September 27, 2010, http://www.ip-watch.org/2010/09/27/the-realities-of-traditional-knowledge-and-patents/; Mangala Hirwade, "Protecting Traditional Knowledge Digitally: A Case Study of TKDL," ed. Anil Chikate and Mangala Hirwade, http://eprints.rclis.org/14020/; Vishwas Chouhan, "Protection of Traditional Knowledge in India by Patent: Legal Aspect," IOSR Journal of Humanities and Social Science 3, no. 1 (2012): 35–42.

36. Lyons, X-Marks, 1–3.

37. Gale Courey Toensing, "Oneida Indian Nation Gets Trust Land," Indian Country Media Network, June 5, 2014, http://indiancountrytodaymedianetwork.com/2014/06/05/oneida-indian-nation-gets-trust-land-finally-155162.

lands in California.[38] I am not saying wealthy settlers who return land are decolonizing. I am saying that some colonizing technology has been hotwired; something scyborg is happening.

The truth is that any return of land is not just due to the good graces and benevolence of wealthy settlers; it is a scyborg possibility foretold by an x-mark. About Hollywood star Johnny Depp's purported promise to buy land for Comanche, Sonny Skyhawk, a Sicangu Lakota actor and founder of American Indians in Film and Television, said, "If it's from the heart, we accept it. If it's not from the heart, we'll accept it anyways."[39]

Developed as weapons of surveillance and assassination, drones are hard to imagine as decolonizing instruments; yet these machines we hate may serve a function before we discard them. Originally a wind-powered device similar to the childhood wind toys of its Afghani creator Massoud Hassani, the Mine Kafon drone "can autonomously map, detect, and detonate land mines" and could contribute to demilitarizing mine-filled lands within a generation.[40] Dynamite, which left Alfred Nobel rich and many dead, and which abetted in U.S. westward imperial expansion, blew up the Elwha and Glines Canyon dams and restored the Elwha River.[41] A giant, autonomous artificial coastline could assist the ocean to clean herself of the great Pacific Garbage

38. Mary Callahan, "Nearly 700 Acres of Sonoma County Coast Protected under Deal with Landowners, Kashia Pomo," *Press Democrat,* October 18, 2015, http://www.pressdemocrat.com/news/4615137-181/nearly -700-acres-of-sonoma?artslide=0.

39. Kristi Eaton, "Reactions to Depp's Wounded Knee Talk," *Newspaper Rock* (blog), July 13, 2013, http://newspaperrock.bluecorncomics .com/2013/07/reactions-to-depps-wounded-knee-talk.html.

40. James Vincent, "This Drone Can Detect and Detonate Land Mines," *The Verge* (blog), July 19, 2016, http://www.theverge.com/2016/7/19/12222104 /landmine-detecting-drone-mine-kafon-drone; http://minekafon.org/.

41. "Restoration of the Elwha River—Olympic National Park (U.S. National Park Service)," https://www.nps.gov/olym/learn/nature /restorationoftheelwha.htm.

Patch.[42] Oysters made "plantable" by farming technologies detoxify the Hudson and so become too poisonous to eat, but because of them, the frogs will return.[43] Wind-powered *strandbeests*—originally devised to restore Dutch beaches—now roam almost autonomous, almost free.[44] Toxic and explosive and wind-willed machine animals, you, scyborg, might read about and feel some odd sense of recognition.

Figure out how technologies operate. Use a wrench. Technologies can be disrupted and reorganized—at least for a machine cycle. Rather than thinking of ourselves as just subjects of those technologies, think about how we are the drones, the explosives, the toxified, the operative parts of those technologies—and ideally, how we might operate on ourselves and other technologies and turn these gears into decolonizing operations.

If this sounds easy and obvious, then my writing has failed you. Listen: you will need to remember this when you are accused of destruction. Attach a pacemaker to the heart of those machines you hate; make it pump for your decolonizing enterprise; let it tick its own countdown. Ask how, and how otherwise, of the colonizing machines. Even when they are dangerous.

42. Rob Speekenbrink, "TEDxDelft 2012 | Performer: Boyan Slat—How the Oceans Can Clean Themselves," TEDxDelft, August 28, 2012, http://www.tedxdelft.nl/2012/08/performer-boyan-how-the-oceans-can-clean-themselves/.

43. "Oyster Research Restoration Project," Hudson River Fund, http://www.hudsonriver.org/?x=orrp.

44. Ian Frazier, "The March of the Strandbeests," *The New Yorker*, September 5, 2011, http://www.newyorker.com/magazine/2011/09/05/the-march-of-the-strandbeests.

Land. And the University
Is Settler Colonial

LAND ACCUMULATION as institutional capital is likely the defining trait of a competitive, modern-day research university. Land is not just an early feature in the establishment of universities. Land is a motor in the financing of universities, enabling many of them to grow despite economic crises. In my own university context during the subprime loan bust of 2008, California campuses expanded facilities construction even while classes were closed, staff furloughed, enrollments frozen, and tuition and fees hiked.[1] One common joke is that "UC" means "Under Construction" rather than "University of California"; similar satirical acronyms exist throughout the research university world. The irony of continued property expansion and revenue generation while enrollments are capped and tuitions balloon has characterized the twenty-first-century university. Land is the keystone of the university, yet land is least likely to be discussed in any critical treatment of it.

Universities do not exist in some abstract academic place. They are built on land, and especially in the North American con-

1. See also Paula Chakravartty and Denise Ferreira da Silva, eds., "Race, Empire, and the Crisis of the Subprime," special issue, *American Quarterly* 64, no. 3 (2012).

text, upon occupied Indigenous lands. From where I write, the California public university system is a land-grant institution. This means that stolen land was (and is) the literal capital used to buy and build one of the largest university systems in the world; the tripartite of California community colleges, California state universities, and the University of California system constitute the largest such public institution in the world (and, arguably, the largest public institution of any sort).

Land-grant institutions were legally born in 1862, when Abraham Lincoln signed the Morrill Act into law. The passage of the Morrill Act is often narrated as a quiet, civilian accomplishment during the U.S. Civil War. Nonetheless, it was truly intimate to war and to the production of a Yankee North American empire. In 1862, seven Southern states seceded from the Union and thus removed from Congress the dissenting votes that had previously blocked the Morrill Act from becoming law. The act gave federal public lands to (Union) states, allotting thirty thousand acres of recently appropriated Indigenous lands for each senator and representative to stake out. States were encouraged to *sell* these "land grants" to raise money for new public universities that would research and educate American settlers in agriculture, science, and mechanical arts. Land is turned into capital for constructing universities for the principal goal of growing industry:[2]

> That all moneys derived from the sale of the lands aforesaid by the States to which the lands are apportioned . . . the moneys so invested shall constitute a perpetual fund, the capital of which shall remain forever undiminished, . . . and the interest of which shall be inviolably appropriated, by each State which may take and claim the benefit of this act, to the endowment, support, and maintenance of at least one college. (Morrill Act, section 4, para. 7)

2. The Morrill Act is still in effect. I use present tense to attend to the contemporary nature of settler colonialism, to insist that our analytics do not refer to settler colonialism as a "past" event.

Land as *capital* and not as *campuses* is an innovation of the land-grant university. That is, states are able to trade, develop, and sell land to fund the construction of public universities. Land as capital incentivized land speculation. For example, New York State acquired its Morrill Act lands in 160-acre denominations, or "scrip," which could be traded privately, even for lands in other states. Most notably, Ezra Cornell, cofounder of Cornell University and of the Western Union Company, traded 532,000 acres of scrip in New York to acquire timber-rich lands in Wisconsin. The "Western Lands," as they were appropriately dubbed, fueled Cornell University from 1865 until the last scrip was finally liquidated in 1935.[3] Therefore land-grant universities are built not only *on* land but also *from* land.

Morrill Act universities are also charged with the research and development of land, particularly for agribusiness. Thus the university system, especially in the westward-expanding empire of the United States, is intimately underwritten as a project of settler colonialism—the seizing of Native land, the conversion of land into capital, the further domestication of "wilderness" into productive agricultural estates, and the research mandate to procure profitable plants from around the world to colonize North American soil. The public university, with its charge to underwrite industry and agribusiness, literally changed the landscape of the Americas:

> The leading object shall be, without excluding other scientific and classical studies, and including military tactics, to teach such branches of learning as are related to agriculture and the mechanic arts, ... in order to promote the liberal and practical education of the industrial classes. (Morrill Act, section 4, para. 1)

The prioritization of settler colonial technologies—agricultural and mechanical engineering, not to mention military tactics—

3. Dewan, "Realities of Traditional Knowledge and Patents in India"; Hirwade, "Protecting Traditional Knowledge Digitally"; Chouhan, "Protection of Traditional Knowledge in India by Patent."

reflects how land-grant universities were commissioned as part of the empire-self-making project of the United States.

The year 1862 also saw the passage of the Homestead Act, which allowed for settlers to apply directly for landownership. Between 1862 and 1934, the federal government granted 1.6 million homesteads, distributing more than 270 million acres—10 percent of all land in the United States—into private (settler) ownership. Homesteading was only officially discontinued in 1976 in the mainland United States and in 1986 in Alaska. The year 1862 also saw the establishment of the Department of Agriculture, and one can see the alchemy of capitalism at work: accumulation of land, conversion of land into capital, conversion of capital into institutions, conversion of land into agribusiness.

In my own University of California context, the state legislature established an Agricultural, Mining, and Mechanical Arts College in 1866,[4] the same year of the Three Knolls Massacre, where settlers killed forty Yahi, including the father of "Ishi, the last Yahi." Also that year, the College Homestead Association purchased 160 acres of Ohlone land in hopes of selling new homesteads to settlers to fund the private College of California. Those lands, along with the Agricultural, Mining, and Mechanical Arts College, would become present-day UC Berkeley. Ironically, "Ishi" became a well-known spectacle for Berkeley anthropologists. After his death, his body was autopsied at the University of California medical school. His body was cremated at a cemetery in Colma, while his brain was shipped to and stored at the Smithsonian in Washington, D.C.—until his remains were finally repatriated back to the Redding Rancheria and Pit River tribe in 2000. Such stories of land appropriations built upon Indigenous vanishings directly haunt the histories of all the UC campuses, whose birth dates march right through the twentieth century: UCLA (1927), UC

4. "A Brief History of the University of California," http://www.ucop .edu/academic-personnel-programs/programs-and-initiatives/faculty -resources-advancement/faculty-handbook-sections/brief-history.html.

Santa Barbara (1958), UC Davis (1959), UC Riverside (1959), UC San Diego (1960), UC San Francisco (1964), UC Santa Cruz (1965), UC Irvine (1965), and UC Merced (2005). There is nothing ancient about this history.

On its 2012 sesquicentennial, the Morrill Act was heavily commemorated throughout the U.S. university system, but perhaps the single organization with the most reason to cheer was the Association of Public and Land-Grant Universities (APLU), "a research, policy, and advocacy organization representing 219 public research universities, land-grant institutions, state university systems, and related organizations." On January 4, 2014, the APLU Executive Committee issued a statement to "strongly oppose the boycott of Israeli academic institutions supported by certain U.S. scholarly organizations," in direct response to the Association for Asian American Studies's (AAAS) April 2013 and the American Studies Association's (ASA) December 2013 resolutions to support the call for boycotts, divestments, and sanctions (BDS) by Palestinian civil society—although neither the scholarly organizations nor Palestine nor the exact boycott is mentioned in the statement.[5]

BDS is built around three demands, specifically, "1. Ending Israel's occupation and colonization of all Arab lands and dismantling the Wall [built around the West Bank and Gaza]; 2. Recognizing the fundamental rights of the Arab-Palestinian citizens of Israel to full equality; 3. And respecting . . . the rights of Palestinian refugees to return to their homes and properties as stipulated in UN resolution 194."[6] According to Palestinian American scholar J. I. Albahri, BDS "is designed to intervene on

5. "APLU Statement in Opposition to Boycott of Israeli Academic Institutions," APLU, January 2, 2014, http://www.aplu.org/news-and-media /News/aplu-statement-in-opposition-to-boycott-of-israeli-academic -institutions; "About APLU," APLU, http://www.aplu.org/page.aspx?pid= 203.

6. "Palestinian Civil Society Call for BDS," BDS Movement, July 9, 2005, https://bdsmovement.net/call.

the specific settler colonial practices of Israel" by exerting international pressure on Israeli institutions.[7]

Shirking the actual words in BDS is the APLU's refusal to engage
public debate—the very cornerstone of free speech. The APLU's
statement nonspecifically refers to "this boycott" as detrimental to
equally nonspecific "critical projects that advance humanity, develop new technologies, and improve health and well-being across
the globe."[8] Some of the discourses deployed by the APLU and other academic voices quick to condemn BDS were that "boycotts are
bad" because "free speech is good." Ironically, the very ineffability
of Palestine reflects a national policy of boycotting open dialogue
about Palestine.

U.S. foreign policy already looks like a boycott of Palestine.
The United States has boycotted the United Nations Educational,
Scientific, and Cultural Organization (UNESCO) assembly since
November 2011, when Palestine was allowed membership into
UNESCO. The United States was by far the largest funder of
UNESCO; by withholding dues of $80 million a year—22 percent
of UNESCO's overall budget—it sent UNESCO into budgetary crisis.[9] Unlike the AAAS and ASA resolutions, *this boycott*—the boycott of Palestine—literally defunds critical projects that "improve
health and well-being across the globe." This boycott is not sub-
mitted for vote or discussion but operates at the level of default
policy—a policy that includes refusals even to name Palestine,
similar to the APLU statement, which would not even name BDS.
Unlike the AAAS and ASA resolutions, the APLU's "boycott of the

7. J. I. Albahri, "Hands Clasped behind Her Back: Palestinian Waiting
on Theories of Change," in Tuck and Yang, *Youth Resistance Research and
Theories of Change,* 169.

8. "APLU Statement in Opposition to Boycott of Israeli Academic
Institutions."

9. Associated Press, "US Loses UNESCO Voting Rights after Stopping
Funds over Palestine Decision," *The Guardian,* November 8, 2013, https://
www.theguardian.com/world/2013/nov/08/us-unesco-voting-funds
-palestine-decision.

boycott" was quickly drafted and signed by six people.[10] It did not solicit votes, feedback, or discussion from its member campuses, which, by the APLU's own claim, "enroll more than 3.8 million undergraduates and 1.2 million graduate students, award over 1 million degrees, employ nearly 1 million faculty and staff, and conduct more than $37 billion in university-based research."[11] The APLU's action perfectly captures how the settler colonial university's investments do not just stem from land seizures of a settler past but are active investments in the very future of settler colonialism.

This chapter cannot deconstruct the complex American desires surrounding Israel and Palestine. However, relevant to this discussion are the similar yet divergent trajectories of the APLU and ASA as university formations—and thus as technological formations that can be repurposed toward decolonizing goals. The APLU was founded in 1887 as a direct consequence of the Morrill Act. The ASA was founded in 1951 as a project of Cold War cultural politics through financial support from the U.S. government— which also endowed multiple professorships in European universities, particularly in Germany and Britain. The dominant origin story of American studies is that it was established as a tool of U.S. jingoism and imperialist apology.[12] From a deterministic view of technology as recapitulating ideology, one might not expect a resolution to support the BDS to emerge from the ASA. That the ASA became a lightning rod for BDS politics was perhaps some-

10. The debates and discussions in the ASA spanned at least seven years, and in an election that attracted 1,252 voters, the largest number of participants in the organization's history, 66.05 percent of voters endorsed the resolution, whereas 30.5 percent of voters voted no and 3.43 percent abstained. The election was a response to the ASA National Council's announcement on December 4 that it supported the academic boycott and, in an unprecedented action to ensure a democratic process, asked its membership for their approval.

11. "About APLU."

12. Allen F. Davis, "The Politics of American Studies," *American Quarterly* 42, no. 3 (1990): 353–74.

thing never predicted by the Cold War machinery that created it. However, from its inception, American studies arguably has had a decolonial tooth in its gear of empire.[13]

The politics of land-grant institutions directs us to think about the work of school beyond curriculum and pedagogy, beyond knowledge production. Universities are land-grabbing, land-transmogrifying, land-capitalizing machines. Universities are giant machines attached to other machines: war machines, media machines, governmental and nongovernmental policy machines. Therefore the terms of the struggle in the university are also over this machinery—deactivating its colonizing operations and activating its contingent decolonizing possibilities.

A decolonizing university is not just about decolonizing the "representational" work of knowledge production that we associate with universities, nor about "decolonizing" the treatment of currently enrolled students in its courses of study. It is about the steam and pistons, the waterworks, the groundworks, the investments, the emplacements, the institutional–governmental–capitalistic rhizomatics of the university. What can we do with this hulking mass of ruins, conduit, fibroids, workhouses, and research facilities built on Indigenous land? What would it take for universities to rematriate land? What would it take for universities to clean water? What would it mean for universities to counteract war making? What would it mean to hotwire the university for decolonizing work? To these machines of decolonial desire, the desire for a third university, this book now turns.

13. James Brown, "Interdisciplinary American Studies and the Cold War: A New, Archival History from the Records of the Library of Congress," paper presented at the annual meeting of the American Studies Association, Albuquerque, N.M., 2008, http://citation.allacademic.com/meta/p_mla_apa _research_citation/2/4/4/7/8/p244780_index.html.

A Third University Exists within the First

IN THIS CHAPTER, I propose a frame for the university in terms of first, second, third, (and fourth) worlds. To do so, I draw from a range of political–intellectual analyses, perhaps the most contemporary of which are the four forms of civil society as analyzed by the project of *México Profundo*.[1] Subcomandante Marcos of the Zapatista Army of National Liberation described the layers of Mexican civil society as Penthouse Mexico, Middle Mexico, Lower Mexico, and Basement Mexico.[2] In the Zaptistas' critique, Basement Mexico is not only a site of dispossession but also a deep well of Indigenous cosmology, wisdom, and sovereignty, *un México profundo*. This is the "fourth," autonomous form of civil society. In this book, I use *fourth world university* as a placeholder for the places of epistemology that are autonomous from the university. In this sense, "fourth worlding" wisdoms are sover-

1. Guillermo Bonfil Batalla, *México Profundo: Una Civilización Negada,* 1st ed. (México, D.F.: Secretaría de Educación Pública/CIESAS, 1987); Gustavo Esteva and Carlos Perez, "The Meaning and Scope of the Struggle for Autonomy," *Latin American Perspectives* 28, no. 2 (2001): 120–48.

2. Marcos and Žiga Vodovnik, *Ya Basta! Ten Years of the Zapatista Uprising: Writings of Subcomandante Insurgente Marcos,* 1st ed. to the United States/United Kingdom (Oakland, Calif.: AK Press, 2004).

eign.[3] Yet they offer decolonial strategies to be carried out within the other three civil societies, even when those strategies are wrapped within the dominant project of statecraft and transnational capital accumulation. We might think of the first and second world universities as the penthouse and middle universities. Inside these universities exists the third world university.

In this regard, I am also drawing from third world feminist conceptualizations that position the "third world" not merely as a site of domination by the Global North over the Global South but also as a crucible of transformative politics and pedagogy.[4] Following other thinkers, I recognize the problematic uses of *third world*. On one hand, it was a signifier for different revolutionary nationalisms in the twentieth century: Juan Perón's "third way" in Argentina and the Cuban Revolution were two such nationalisms that aspired to challenge Cold War binaries that revolved around the competing empires of the United States and the USSR. On the other hand, the third world is a warrant for nongovernmental organizations to operate as self-stylized humanitarian ventures and also for-profit corporations to dress up as charities.[5] My choice to use *third world* is meant to be problematic. Any decolonizing proj-

3. My use of *fourth world* is not intended as a reference to "fourth world cinema," and I am not equating Indigenous worlds with the "fourth world." Admittedly, my use of the fourth world as a source of wisdom is a bit romanticized. However, I do so not for the sake of romance but for the purpose of asserting that some forms of knowledge and learning ought to refuse the university—following Indigenous writers Audra Simpson, Eve Tuck, and Sandy Grande. Community and Indigenous knowledges are already prefigured in the academy as folk/superstitious, as unscientific, as effeminate, or, in the most colonial ways, as "data" to then be appropriated as objects to be reinterpreted and renarrated back to you. Therefore I am using *fourth world* to assert the value of those knowledges, without turning them into valued commodities. I am using *fourth world* to make space.

4. See Chandra Talpade Mohanty, "Under Western Eyes: Feminist Scholarship and Colonial Discourses," *Feminist Review,* no. 30 (1988): 61–88.

5. See Albahri, "Hands Clasped behind Her Back"; Gilmore, afterword, 230–33.

ect of the third world university should be a problematized one, in much the same way as revolutionary nationalisms and international aid should be problematized.

Most directly, a third world university references the organizing by the Third World Liberation Front in the late 1960s and early 1970s to found a Third World College. These events reached an apex in the 1968–69 San Francisco State Strike; at 167 days, it was the longest student strike in U.S. history.

However, I find that the most precise analogy for a third world university, both materially and symbolically, is offered by Third Cinema. Glen Mimura explains:

> First Cinema, in this framework, is the cinema of the studio systems—Hollywood preeminently, but also Bollywood and any other capitalist film industry that, regardless of its formal and thematic diversity, is characterized by an ultimate commitment to corporate profits and mass entertainment. Second Cinema, comprising independent or "art" cinema, may indeed offer meaningful challenges to studio system productions; however, its defining pursuit of questions of art and aesthetics displaces the possibility of sustained, radical critique, and thereby remains circumscribed "within the system." In contrast, Third Cinema defines itself fundamentally as a political project—as a democratic, participatory, socialist cinema that seeks to challenge and provoke the collective consciousness of its viewers toward the revolutionary transformation of society.
>
> To be sure, no mode of cinema is completely distinct, autonomous; each mode appropriates or contains within itself elements of the other two. . . . To paraphrase an oft-quoted line by Trinh Minh-ha, there is a Third Cinema in every First and Second Cinema, and vice versa.[6]

6. Glen M. Mimura, *Ghostlife of Third Cinema: Asian American Film and Video* (Minneapolis: University of Minnesota Press, 2009), 30. Mimura lists notable filmmaker collectives that explicitly aligned themselves with Third Cinema: Grupo Cine Liberación; Black Arts movement in London (Sankofa and the Black Audio Film and Video Collective); Amber Films in Newcastle, England; Appalshop in Appalachia, Whitesburg, Kentucky; Third World Newsreel in New York City; Visual Communications in Los Angeles, California. All six were founded in the late 1960s. Ibid., 33.

Materially, both cinema and the university require a high concentration of capital. Each industry requires a willing civil society of moviegoers and university-goers, physical theaters and physical campuses, digital videos and digital learning platforms. Whereas cinema's investments are mostly liquid capital, the university's investments are land and debt. Cinema's horizon of consumption is the total population of visually abled people. Likewise, the university, though historically elitist, has expanded its horizons toward the total debt-enabled population—to be discussed shortly. Pedagogically, cinema and university perform complementary roles in the production of the symbolic order. Cinema is a key industry in the production of "commonsense knowledge," as compared to the university's production of legitimated knowledge. Whereas cinema accumulates images for a visual grammar book, the university accumulates scholarship for an epistemological grammar book.

Through this analogy of Third Cinema, we can describe the university as an amalgam of first, second, and third world formations. Substituting "university" for "cinema" and rephrasing Mimura's description of cinema, we derive a reasonable definition for third university:

> *The first world university is the academic–industrial complex: "research-ones" preeminently, but also commercial universities and any other corporate academic enterprise that, regardless of its formal and thematic diversity, is characterized by an ultimate commitment to brand expansion and accumulation of patent, publication, and prestige. The second world university, comprising independent or "liberal arts" colleges, may indeed offer meaningful challenges to the academic–industrial complex, and could be said to be a democratic and participatory academy that seeks to challenge and provoke the critical consciousness of its students toward self-actualization. However, its defining pursuit of questions of art, humanities, and a libertarian mode of critical thinking displaces the possibility of sustained, radical critique and thereby remains circumscribed "within the ivory tower." In contrast, the third world university defines itself fundamentally as a decolonial project—as an interdisciplinary, transnational, yet vocational university that equips its students with skills toward the applied practice of decolonization.*

> *To be sure, no mode of university is completely distinct, autonomous; each mode appropriates or contains within itself elements of the other two. There is a third university in every first and second university, and vice versa.*

The first world university accumulates through dispossession. The second world university "liberates" through liberalism. The third world university breaks faith from its own machinery by inspiriting the academic automaton with a fourth world soul.

The First University Accumulates

The first world university charges fees and grants degrees. This university is a machine of accumulation and expansion, increasingly carried out by neoliberal mechanisms that tie the production of knowledge to grant RFPs and revenue-generating enterprises. In the United States, it includes the R-1s that typically boast PhD programs and D-1 sports teams. Its big moneymakers are STEM degrees, MBAs, and MDs; extension programs; online classrooms; international student fees; and distance degrees.[7] First world universities keep count of their Nobel laureates and count on large research grants from the Departments of Energy, Agriculture, Defense, and, increasingly, Homeland Security.

While I was writing this to you, Janet Napolitano, the former U.S. secretary of Homeland Security, assumed her new post as the twentieth president of the University of California system, the first woman to occupy the office. The revolving door between institutions of policing, bordering, surveillance, incarceration, illegalization, militarization, and schooling is not new. Indeed, in San Diego, where I am based, Alan Bersin was superintendent of public schools from 1998 to 2005, after three years of running U.S.–Mexican border law enforcement for Attorney General Janet Reno

7. In terms of license/degree programs for profit, vocational and commercial universities represent a type of market share in the first world university.

under President Clinton. After his stint governing schools, Bersin governed the border (again) in 2009, this time for the Obama administration, working as "border czar" under Janet Napolitano, then Homeland Security secretary, now UC president. However, it would be a misguided comparison to describe the bodies of faculty and students as analogous to the bodies of detainees and deportees and migrants and suspectees. It is not analogous power but technologies of power that recirculate in these imperial triangles, for example, debt financing, neoliberal market policies, information systems, managing noncitizen populations, land development. If we consider triangular connections between war abroad and refugee management within, antiblackness and the maintenance of black fungibility and accumulation, and militarization and Indigenous erasure throughout empire, then we can understand why the governors of war and the governors of schools can have similar résumés, without pretending that the governed suffer through identical conditions.

Of particular importance to the first world university are technologies of accumulation through colonial contract: the procuring of state resources in order to govern, expand, or research and develop. In this respect, a former director of any federal department is eminently qualified to be a university president. The first world university also accumulates through debt, that is, through the entire business of debt production and management: loaning, borrowing, repaying, defaulting. This ability to turn anyone into a debtor is what fuels the first university toward inclusion. The desires of people—especially Global South people—for meaningful education gets attached by a chain-drive into the desire of debt. We become educated by becoming indebted.

As Jean Anyon noted, one in every nine young people living in poverty in the United States *has a college degree,* and nearly half are attending or have attended college.[8] In high-poverty areas, there are

---

8. Jean Anyon, *Radical Possibilities: Public Policy, Urban Education,*

not enough jobs to match college degrees. There are not enough jobs for high school grads. There are not enough jobs. As education-al researchers have pointed out, "schools matter, but they're not all that matters."[9] The rhetoric of college-for-all has redirected public attention away from resolving issues of poverty and toward specu-lating on test scores. On average, a white person without a college degree has more wealth than a Black or Latino person with a col-lege degree; this phenomenon is not well understood and has yet to be carefully studied, but mainstream pundits have already decided that the racial "wealth gap" is curable through higher education.[10] Without functional wealth, or what Thomas Shapiro calls "trans-formative assets" used to offset the opportunity costs of college tu-ition and underemployment as a student, higher education is ob-tained at a very poor exchange rate.[11]

After mortgages, student loans are the largest form of debt now in the United States. Indeed, families are mortgaging their homes (homeownership being the material definition of "middle class") for children to attend college (the college degree being the sym-bolic definition of "middle class"). This is a bitter irony of dispos-session through debt, whereby college-sending families lose the materiality of the middle class to obtain middle-class status.

Moreover, underrepresented minority students disproportion-ately enter community-oriented professions where unemploy-ment is high and wages are low. Georgetown University's Center

and a New Social Movement, Critical Social Thought (New York: Routledge, 2005).

9. Pedro Noguera, "Accept It: Poverty Hurts Learning: Schools Matter, but They're Not All That Matters," *Daily News,* September 2, 2010, http://www.nydailynews.com/opinion/accept-poverty-hurts-learning-schools-matter-matters-article-1.439586#ixzz2pfMZFFfk.

10. Sharmila Choudhury, "Racial and Ethnic Differences in Wealth and Asset Choices," *Social Security Bulletin* 64 (2002): 1–15.

11. Thomas M. Shapiro, *The Hidden Cost of Being African American: How Wealth Perpetuates Inequality* (New York: Oxford University Press, 2004).

on Education and the Workforce reports that the majors with the lowest earnings include social work, human services and community organizations, early childhood education, and counseling psychology, just below visual performing arts, studio arts, and drama and theater arts.[12]

The university system has expanded under the premise that workers, and the families of students, will take on debt. With accountability regimes like No Child Left Behind and Race for the Top and the neoliberal positioning of education as a panacea for all social ills, the change we see entering the twenty-first century is that the expanding academic–industrial complex has its cross hairs on the *total* youth population as its biopolitical target. Thus the implication of the worker as consumer, or, more accurately, the debtor as consumer of the university, likens it to the cinema's horizon of the total seeing population as its audience.

However, the first world university's most expansive desire is for a global empire of satellite campuses or "outpost universities":

> Ardently pursued by university presidents as strategic and legacy plans, the race to be the global university has become an "educational gold rush." This is tellingly mapped out by the geography of its expansion. Countries such as China, India, Singapore, and the United Arab Emirates are targeted as feasible sites because of their oil wealth as well as industrial and population growth.[13]

Eng-Beng Lim analyzes this trend through such examples as King Abdullah University of Science and Technology (KAUST), a new graduate university in Saudi Arabia with an instant US$10 billion endowment and that has partnered with Stanford, UT Austin,

12. Anthony P. Carnevale, Ban Cheah, and Jeff Strohl, "Hard Times: College Majors, Unemployment, and Earnings: Not All College Degrees Are Created Equal," 2012, https://repository.library.georgetown.edu/handle/10822/559308.
13. Eng-Beng Lim, "Performing the Global University," *Social Text 101* 27, no. 4 (2009): 27.

and UC Berkeley. According to the *New York Times,* without the "post-9/11 visa problems of traveling to America,"

> at Education City in Doha, Qatar's capital, they can study medicine at Weill Medical College of Cornell University, international affairs at Georgetown, computer science and business at Carnegie Mellon, fine arts at Virginia Commonwealth, engineering at Texas A&M, and soon, journalism at Northwestern.[14]

Lim dubs places like Education City "the return of the colonial metropole." But, in analyzing the likes of NYU's Tisch School of the Arts Asia in Singapore, Lim points out that the colonial metropole is not simply a science and technology magnet; arts and humanities departments have also looked toward the global university to escape budgetary decline through capitalist expansion. This leads us to the second world university.

The Second University Critiques

The second world university, like Second Cinema, is marked by its investments in critical theory, that is, the diverse work of the Frankfurt School in critiquing media and capitalist systems in the "West" that emerged out of World War II. Two threads of critical theory run through academia in the arts and humanities, on one hand, and the social sciences, on the other. *Literary critical theory* focuses on the deconstruction of texts for their underlying meanings, whereas *social theory* focuses on domination within social systems, usually from a neo-Marxist frame.[15] At least ideologically, the second world university is committed to the transformation of society *through critique,* through a deconstruction of systems of

14. Tamar Lewin, "Universities Rush to Set Up Outposts Abroad," *New York Times,* February 10, 2008, A1.

15. Jürgen Habermas, *Knowledge and Human Interests* (Boston: Beacon Press, 1971); Raymond Allen Morrow and Carlos Alberto Torres, *Social Theory and Education: A Critique of Theories of Social and Cultural Reproduction* (Albany: SUNY Press, 1995).

power, and in this way offers fundamental analyses for any third world university curriculum. Yet its hidden curriculum reflects the material conditions of higher education—fees, degrees, expertise, and the presumed emancipatory possibilities of the mind—and reinscribes academic accumulation.

Usually, when traditionalists speak with nostalgia for the idealized university of old, the library counter in the sky where Kant and Hegel and Freire study together, this is the second world university. We are familiar with it; in the United States, it often houses the Marxist scholars, the ethnic studies formations, women's studies, gender studies, and American studies. To borrow some rhetoric from Gayatri Spivak, it is the house of the hegemonic radical, the postcolonial ghetto neighborhood within the university metropolis.

One of the tautological traps of the second world university is mistaking its personalized pedagogy of self-actualization for decolonial transformation. When people say "another university is possible," they are more precisely saying that "a second university is possible," and they are often imagining second world utopias, where the professor ceases to profess, where hierarchies disappear, where all personal knowledges are special, and, in other words, none are. Their assumption is that people will "naturally" produce freedom, and freedom's doppelganger is critical consciousness. They are rarely talking about a university that rematriates land, that disciplines scholar-warriors rather than "liberating" its students, that repurposes the industrial machinery, that supports insurrectionary nationalisms as problematic antidotes to imperialist nationalism, that acts upon financial systems rather than just critiquing them, that helps in the accumulation of third world power rather than simply disavowing first world power, that is a school-to-community pipeline, not a community-to-school pipeline. In short, "another university is possible," so far, hasn't made possible a third world university.

The second world university announces itself through nostalgia. Sara Ahmed describes this as "an academic world [that] can be idealised in being mourned as a lost object; a world where dons get to decide things; a world imagined as democracy, as untroubled by the whims and wishes of generations to come."[16] This nostalgia can be futuristic, indeed, the dons are imagining themselves a permanent future in a white academic pantheon. This is similar to settler futurity, which is always nostalgic for its own current power, fearful that it may come to pass.

The second world university is a pedagogical utopia. Its horizons are still total in that its end goal is a utopia that everyone should and can attend. This liberal expansion rests materially on the continued accumulation of fees, debt, and land by its big baby turned big baby daddy, the first world university.[17] Nonetheless, second world critique does inform third world work. As Denise da Silva has often said, "we cannot stay in the work of critique, but we must go *through* critique to get to the work." Through critique, and the dirty work that follows it, we might find some machinery useful for a third world.

A Third University Strategizes

The third world university defines itself against the first and second but is probably made up of their scrap material. Its aim is decolonization, but its attempts at decolonization can range broadly from nationalistic bids for membership into the family of nations to transnational forms of cooperation to local movements for autonomy to Indigenous sovereignty; these are particularistic strategies of anticolonial and decolonial projects that are not necessarily aligned with one another. By necessity, the third world university

16. Sara Ahmed, "Against Students," *Feministkilljoys* (blog), June 25, 2015, https://feministkilljoys.com/2015/06/25/against-students/.
17. The first world is the "big baby" of the second world university. See the previous chapter on the Morrill Act and land-grant universities as engineering schools born out of more classical universities. The first world university was the baby and is now the sugar daddy.

teaches first world curricula: medicine where hospitals are needed for sovereign bodies; engineering where wastewater systems are needed for sovereign lands; legal studies where the law is a principal site of decolonial struggle; agricultural science where seeds are being patented, modified, and sterilized; food studies where the land mass-produces net export crops but there is a food shortage; enterprise where capital is needed for sovereign economies. It teaches a second world critique, because only through critique can the colonial code be cracked. Like Third Cinema, the third world university "does not simply incorporate or quote these sources, but actively reinvents them through their appropriations . . . to synthesize these disparate sources into not only a coherent discourse but a far-reaching, transformative radical project."[18] It is part of the machinery of the university, a part that works by breaking down and producing counters to the first and second machineries. As a strategic reassemblage of first world parts, it is not a decolonized university but a decolonizing one. But it still produces. It probably still charges fees and grants degrees.

What does the third world university feel like? You might find this part unsatisfying. I refuse to offer a utopic description for a strategic decolonizing machine (for utopias, go to the second world). I hope you make this same refusal. However, I am sure that many readers are involved in university projects with decolonial desires to implement change pragmatically, readers who have appropriated university resources to synthesize a transformative, radical project. These formations may be personal, even solitary; they may be small working groups of like-minded university workers, research centers, degree programs, departments, even colleges. Te Whare Wānanga o Awanuiārangi in Aoteroa might be the clearest example of a decolonizing university formation.[19] If

18. Mimura, *Ghostlife of Third Cinema,* 32.

19. Whare Wānanga o Awanuia-rangi, "Prospectus," http://docs .wananga.ac.nz/split_document.php?subfolder=&doc=Prospectus%202016 .pdf.

we consider the Cuban Latin American School of Medicine as a university from which decolonizing work sometimes emerges—as it has trained more than twenty-five thousand physicians from eighty-four countries in Latin America, the Caribbean, North America, Africa, Asia, and Oceania to return to their home communities where doctors and medical care are scarce—then some third world university formations can operate at the scale of state apparatuses.[20] However, besides literal "third world" formations like Escuela Latinoamericana de Medicina (ELAM), and explicitly decolonizing universities like Te Whare Wānanga o Awanuiārangi, the third world university also appears contemporaneously within first world universities.

As an insightful example, Ta-Nehisi Coates describes Howard University and the Mecca as imbricating and coinciding institutions:

> I was admitted to Howard University, but formed and shaped by The Mecca. These institutions are related but not the same. Howard University is an institution of higher education, concerned with the LSAT, magna cum laude, and Phi Beta Kappa. The Mecca is a machine, crafted to capture and concentrate the dark energy of all African peoples and inject it directly into the student body.

Coates goes on to root the power of the machine Mecca in the reassembly of Howard University's transhistorical networks of Black, governmental, literary, revolutionary power and the power of place:

> The Mecca derives its power from the heritage of Howard University, which in Jim Crow days enjoyed a near-monopoly on black talent. And whereas most other historically black schools were scattered like forts in the great wilderness of the old Confederacy, Howard was in Washington, D.C.—Chocolate City—and thus in proximity

20. "Historia de La ELAM," http://instituciones.sld.cu/elam /historia-de-la-elam/; Robert Huish and John M. Kirk, "Cuban Medical Internationalism and the Development of the Latin American School of Medicine," *Latin American Perspectives* 34, no. 6 (2007): 77–92.

to bother federal power and black power. The result was an alumni and professorate that spanned genre and generation—Charles Drew, Amiri Baraka, Thurgood Marshall, Ossie Davis, Doug Wilder, David Dinkins, Lucille Clifton, Toni Morrison, Kwame Ture. The history, the location, the alumni combined to create The Mecca.[21]

This remarkable list of Howard University notables represents a fairly divergent constellation of ideologies; David Dinkins, former mayor of New York City, and Kwame Turé of the All-African Peoples Revolutionary Party provide one example of a stark contrast. Yet in the machine of the Mecca, their individual and collective Blackness comes to mean something different in assemblage with one another. As an historically Black college or university (HBCU), Howard University is already an alternative university universe. The Mecca produces yet a third reality, and it does so by reassembling Howard's histories of power, race, and place.

To call these efforts a third university is not to say that they are in political solidarity with one another but rather to call their decolonial possibilities into existence. More precisely, we call forth a contingent collaboration across all these efforts—a transnational, multicampus, multiscalar self-awareness. It is an AI emerging. The analytic work here is to consider how the third world university emerges out of the first, in our respective locations. The political work is to assemble our efforts with a decolonizing spirit and an explicit commitment to decolonization that can be the basis of transnational collaborations and transhistorical endurance.

To Assemble a Decolonizing-Works, We Can Learn from Black Film-Works

Making movies is an apt metaphor for making movement in and through the university. Moviemaking takes place at multiple scales, from individual works of single movies to assembling "works" in

21. Ta-Nehisi Coates and Ta-Nehisi Coates, *Between the World and Me* (Melbourne: Text Publishing Company, 2015), 40.

another sense of "ironworks" and "waterworks." Film-works are the places, premises, and machinery needed to make movies: from small studios to film industries. It is a good way to envision assembling the works of a decolonizing university.

Zeinabu Davis's insightful documentary film *Spirits of Rebellion* reveals the scales and scopes of Black filmmaking works by tracing the contours of what some have termed the LA Rebellion—Black radical filmmakers like Julie Dash, Charles Burnett, Larry Clarke, Haile Gerima, Barbara McCullough, Jamaa Fanaka, Ben Caldwell, Billy Woodberry, Shirikiana Aina, and O. Funmilayo Makarah whose work created a shared legacy of study at the UCLA Film School from the 1960s to the 1980s. Davis herself is part of this genealogy, and her own work marks a continuation, a memory, and an evolution of this legacy as well as the larger tradition of Black film. *Spirits of Rebellion* covers the nuances of their filmic stories and the art of creating Black representational power out of a Hollywood overdetermined form.

What stuck with me through the stories in Davis's documentary were the coincidental linkages between filmmakers, the collaborations necessary for making a film, the materiality of communication technologies, the copyright somersaults in using images and sound, the funding not just to make films but to have them shown, the legal and capital juggernaut of a Hollywood machine that Black filmmakers have to subvert. And all of the filmmakers in Davis's documentary speak to the space-making work of Teshome Gabriel, UCLA professor and scholar of Third Cinema. His efforts were instrumental in composing a third worlding film factory.

Films are not just texts. Films are enterprises. Certainly the products of filmmaking are cinematic texts that can be "read" just like any other literary work—for their signifying meaning, for their impact on existing systems of representation, for the ways that communities and audiences take up the text. However, films are enterprises, requiring money, machines, casts and crews, networks of distribution, and critical audiences who discuss the films.

Donald Glover, speaking about his 2016 FX network show *Atlanta*, described how he organized an all-Black writers' room, all ATLiens, all without Hollywood-esque writers' rooms experiences:

> I did it in my house where I was recording music and also doing the show. We called it the Factory. And we worked out of the Factory.[22]

For Glover to do the representational work of a show whose "thesis . . . was to make people feel black," he also had to assemble a Black enterprise of Black people and Black bricks and mortar.[23] His house as cinematic factory fostered the organic intimacy he envisioned for his show.

Film movements are multiscalar endeavors. One might think about how making an independent short film is one scale. Making a Black film industry is another scale. Consider what the necessary collaborations are for making

- a single film,
- a body of work,
- a film production studio,
- a Black film industry,
- a distribution network for theatrical releases, or
- a Black film movement.

Assembling a decolonizing university is also a multiscalar endeavor. We might ask what the necessary collaborations are for making

22. Rodney Carmichael, "Donald Glover's Real Rap on 'Atlanta,'" *Creative Loafing Atlanta* (blog), August 29, 2016, http://www.clatl.com /culture/article/20831904/donald-glovers-real-rap-on-atlanta.

23. Melanie McFarland, "Inside 'Atlanta' with Donald Glover: 'The Thesis behind the Show Was to Make People Feel Black,'" *Salon*, August 31, 2016, http://www.salon.com/2016/08/31/inside-atlanta-with-donald-glover -the-thesis-behind-the-show-was-to-make-people-feel-black/.

- a single project with a decolonizing aspect,
- a body of decolonizing works,
- a decolonizing production studio,
- a decolonizing industry,
- a network of decolonizing organisms, or
- a decolonizing university movement.

Black film is Black assemblage in flight.

> It is a living thing, Black cinema. It is a living thing that has endured. It has survived under duress since the beginning of the last century with no help, with no tools, with no focus, with no attention, with no water, with no sunlight. And still the images have been made by people long before us. So I do think there are beautiful things that are happening in the space, because there has always been.[24]

The very existence of the preceding quote by filmmaker Ava DuVernay is itself an aperture into the living thing of Black cinema, into its transhistorical timelines and multiscalar assemblages. In this instance, DuVernay is speaking to *Another Round,* a podcast hosted by Heben Nigatu and Tracy Clayton, the Black female creators, hosts, and writers of the show.[25] They are interviewing DuVernay about her forthcoming projects: *13th,* a Netflix documentary on the advent of modern slavery through mass incarceration as generated by the Thirteenth Amendment, and *Queen Sugar,* a dramatic series about a Louisiana family, to be broadcast on the Oprah Winfrey Network (OWN). With a Black podcast audience surrounding her, the Oscar-nominated Hollywood film *Selma* be-

24. Tracy Clayton and Heben Nigatu, "Two Dollars and a Paperclip," *Another Round* (Podcast), September 13, 2016.

25. Adding still more gears, Nigatu and Clayton came up from new media spaces such as BlackTwitter and blogs such as *MadameNoir* and *TheRoot* (founded by Henry Louis Gates Jr.). *Another Round* lives on BuzzFeed.com, one of the single most influential media shapers on the Internet (and thus in mass culture), a site that explicitly functions without a core demographic but through lateral and multiple networks.

hind her, a digital streaming Netflix documentary ahead of her, and a serial drama to be broadcast on a television channel owned by one of the wealthiest Black women of all time, DuVernay is in this moment a rider and a rewriter of Black cinematic assemblage in motion.[26]

Black assemblage involves the modding of technologies raked together by the witch's broom. YouTube, podcasts, blogs, Twitter feeds, digital streaming services, crowdfunding campaigns, are new technologies commandeered by a collaboration of organisms already-readied by producing bodies of works sometimes within first world systems. These collaborations meant that Pharrell's YouTube channel could host *Awkward Black Girl,* that Oprah would televise DuVernay, that podcasts and Twitter hashtags might become Black.

The witch's flight might fashion landing pads out of First Cinema, yet it is always poised to fly away from them. She can "walk into meetings and talk with my studio partners now with a sense of freedom," DuVernay says, because she can always fly away.[27] Her ever-ready refusal of First Cinema is a stance roote in

---

26. The year 2016 is a also year that has seen the "Blackening" of mainstream media—from late-night talk show hosts Larry Wilmore (now canceled) and Noah Trevor to black Marvel superhero Luke Cage on Netflix to successful comedy serials *Blackish* (ABC), *Atlanta* (FX), and *Insecure* (HBO) with Issa Rae—mainstream productions with almost no white cast members. Prior to her HBO deal, Rae got attention as creator, writer, actor, and producer of the YouTube series *Awkward Black Girl,* which went viral enough for a second season premier on record producer Pharrell's YouTube channel iamOTHER. For the surreal dark comedy *Atlanta,* Donald Glover, who acted in *Community* and wrote for NBC's *30 Rock* and also raps as Childish Gambino, similarly absorbed all roles—executive producer, writer, director, executive music producer, and star.

27. DuVernay herself has risen to fame from her 2015 Oscar-nominated film *Selma,* the first film directed by a Black woman to be nominated for an Academy Award—although DuVernay herself was not nominated, during a year that spawned the much-discussed viral hashtag #OscarsSoWhite created by Black Twitter activist, writer, and former lawyer April Reign.

self-determination: "It's because I always know I can make something on two dollars and a paperclip. Always. Always."[28]

Filmmaking is collaborative but not democratic. Most films, even independent ones, require a crew of makers, seek investments by producers, need actors. Films are made collectively, yet generally hierarchically (not usually "democratically"), by a gang of folks who unevenly control the film through their invested cash, their supply and operation of video or film equipment, the coordination of schedules, their scriptwriting and their improvisation. Maybe there is a single director. Maybe creative decisions are born more collaboratively. One ought to be a little agnostic about the value of democracy if one wants to make a film.

When building a decolonizing machine out of colonizing scraps, we ought to ask, what are the types of organizational structures to get it done? What organizational structures do we think we are supposed to have? Why do we think that way?

Universities can certainly be called hierarchical, but such a critique is an incomplete analysis. An evolved colonizing machine, like any code, is not simply hierarchical. If it were, it would not be efficient—there are multiple flows of commands, some hierarchical, some lateral, some "organic" in the sense of emergence.

One ought to be a little agnostic about democracy when inside a colonizing machine. And alternatives to democracy exist. We might think of various Indigenous forms of governance such as elderships or matrilineal land stewardship. We might think about hip-hop governance, or even revolutionary organizations, as a form of relation-based organizing.

A Black film movement is ideologically diverse. What is in common for a Black film movement, I want to say, is a love for

28. Clayton and Nigatu, "Two Dollars and a Paperclip."

Black life and for Blackness. This love functions like gravity; it is everywhere, operating on all things. But it manifests differently in interactions big and small—planetary in scale or intimate. It is not always your friend, and it can lead to plummets, but isn't flying just a falling heart with wings?[29] It is the witch's flight, not linear genealogy, that connects decolonizing work. An effective decolonizing university assemblage must be ideologically diverse; it must have different and differing parts that work. A decolonizing university has only to share that love for Black life, for Indigenous worldings, for their futures.

Axioms about the Third University

I list below axioms for third university actualities. If we consider that a decolonizing university exists already amid the colonial, and that it takes many formations at multiple scales—from the personal to the institutional to the national—then we can start to ascertain the premises for its existence. Axioms should be flexible enough to build multiple formations and to accommodate contradictions, while clear enough to catch the decolonial desires that inspirit these formations. I call them axioms not so much because they are self-evident or irrefutable. Rather, they are axioms in the second sense of the word: propositions upon which a structure, in this case, a decolonizing university, can be built.

1. It already exists. It is assembling. It assembles within the first and second universities.
2. Its mission is decolonization.
3. It is strategic. Its possibilities are made in the first world university.
4. It is timely, and yet its usefulness constantly expires.
5. It is vocational, in the way of the first world university.

29. "The work of wings / was always freedom, fastening / one heart to every falling thing." Li-Young Lee, "One Heart."

6. It is unromantic. And it is not worthy of your romance.

7. It is problematic. In all likelihood, it charges fees and grants degrees.

8. It is not the fourth world.

9. It is anti-utopian. Its pedagogical practices may be disciplining and disciplinary. A third world university is less interested in *decolonizing the university* and more in operating as a *decolonizing university.*

10. It is a machine that produces machines. It assembles students into scyborgs. It assembles decolonizing machines out of scrap parts from colonial technology. It makes itself out of assemblages of the first and second world universities. To the degree that it accomplishes these assemblages, it is effective.

You, a Scyborg

A 2013 TALK BY RODERICK FERGUSON, a foundational intellectual in queer of color critique, inaugurated A Black Studies Project at UC San Diego. He pointed out that the alleged demise of revolutionary thought after the 1970s was overstated by tracing how the third world demands of revolutionary groups in the 1960s and early 1970s were taken up and transformed by the queer of color left, through the development of the Third World Gay Revolution out of the whiter Gay Liberation Front. Ferguson's purpose was not to narrate a history of socialism, nor of revolution, but rather to express the way that queer desire composes desiring machines that reconstruct institutions (and radical organizations too). Queer of color sexuality was not a "natural" political identity and, furthermore, not automatically a "revolutionary" one, and certainly not one recognized as such by people of color. Rather, it became so through many gears rubbing against each other—bodies, literally, rubbing against each other. Ferguson calls these rubbings "associations," that is, the radical idea that all social texts should be open for revision through unexpected contacts, transmissions, and queer translations (Ferguson here is drawing from Roland Barthes). Through these associations of rubbings, frictions, and greasings of gears, new formations come into play. Queer of color not only became revolutionary but became a revolutionary that was previously unrecognized. In so doing, queer of color radicalism also queered the revolutionary platforms of the third world liberation movements.[1]

It is in Ferguson's frame of queer desiring machines that I consider the scyborg (by associating with and deviating a bit from Donna Haraway's formulation of the cyborg) as the agentive body within the institutional machinery. If we think of the university as a machine that is the composite of many other machines, these machines are never perfect loyalists to colonialism—in fact, they are quite disloyal. They break down and produce and travel in unexpected lines of flight—flights that are at once enabled by the university yet irreverent of that mothership of a machine. This same disloyalty applies to the machined people, you. And thus there's some hope, the hope of the scyborg. Organisms in the machinery are scyborgian: as students, staff, faculty, alumni, and college escapees, technologies of the university have been grafted onto you. Your witch's flight pulls bits of the assemblage with you and sprays technology throughout its path.

The agency of the scyborg is precisely that it is a reorganizer of institutional machinery; it subverts machinery against the master code of its makers; it rewires machinery to its own intentions. It's that elliptical gear that makes the machine work (for freedom sometimes) by helping the machine (of unfreedom) break down. The lopsided bot, the scyborg, the queer gear with a g-limp—if there is anything to fear and to hope for in the university, it could be you, and it could be me.

Scyborgs have made a third university. The scyborg is essential in producing the third world university. The scyborg is machined person, technologically enhanced by legitimated knowledge and

---

1. Ferguson's book *The Re-order of Things* (Minneapolis: University of Minnesota Press, 2012) details the possibilities and complicities, the revolution of appropriations, and the appropriation of the revolution in the university.

stamped with the university's brand. S-he is the perfect masculine expression of education: an autonomous individual who will
reproduce the logics of the university without being told. The
scyborg is the university's colonial hope. Albert Memmi describes
being a Tunisian Jew at the Sorbonne in the 1950s, wondering
whether he would be allowed to take his exams. "It is not a right,"
said the president of the exams jury. "It is a hope.... Let us say that
it is a colonial hope."[2] Scyborgs are creatures of colonial desire:
please be successful, be pretty, be human. The scyborg's privilege
is a manifestation of the first world university's noblesse oblige.
Thus a successful scyborg proves that the university is ethical.
However, on the flip side, the scyborg is a source of colonial anx-
iety: please do not fail us, reject us, betray us. The scyborg has hir
desires too. Hirs is a decolonial hope. S-he is never a completely
loyal colonialist and can often be caught in the basement library,
building the third world university.

To recognize the scyborg, I return to the three examples of colonial schools in Kenya, North America, and the Philippines. I do
so to ask that we recognize the nineteenth- and twentieth-century
scyborgs that Christian missions, the U.S. Army, and other colonial
machines might have created by accident.

I opened this book with Ngũgĩ wa Thiong'o's memoirs of Alliance
High School and wartime Kenya. The importance of starting with
a Black example, and an African example, is to choose a starting
point that does not disaggregate Indigeneity and Blackness in the
conversations about colonialism, even though the modes of operation of colonialism upon the Black and the Indigenous are very
divergent.

At Alliance High School, wa Thiong'o was inspired by *Oliver
Twist*, in part out of identification with the story boy's hunger;
in part, perhaps, he aspired to be Charles Dickens. If so, I believe he accomplished it. However, what the Dickens he became

2. Memmi, *The Colonizer and the Colonized*, 4.

is not something that missionary schools could have recognized. He published his first novel in English while at the University of Leeds in 1964. Returning to Kenya, he organized the highly successful but politically explicit theater production of his 1977 play *Ngaahika Ndeenda* (I will marry when I want), which was shut down by the Kenyatta regime. Wa Thiong'o was imprisoned for a year in the Kamiti Maximum Security Prison. There he wrote the first modern novel in the Gĩkũyũ language, *Caitaani mũtharaba-Inĩ* (Devil on the cross), on prison-issued toilet paper.

Luther Standing Bear was one of the first students at Carlisle Industrial School for Indians when it opened in 1879 and, indeed, a model student who looked up to the founder, Captain "kill-the-Indian-save-the-man" Pratt. He even became a recruiter for the school. However, he went on to oppose the Dawes Act that privatized Indian land held in common; to argue for bilingual education for Native children; and to challenge the paradigms of property, Eurocentric history, and assimilation—arguments and alliances that successfully brought about the Indian Reorganization Act of 1934, which officially reversed the Dawes Act and assimilationist schooling and provided pathways for tribes to reestablish sovereignty and tribal government. Troy Richardson, drawing from Gerald Vizenor, writes that Standing Bear's thoughts and deeds suggest a "shadow curriculum" of a deep sovereignty beyond their immediate referents in the (English) world. "Shadows are possibilities, neither empty nor over-determined by words or referents but instances of possibilities."[3] For such aviators of Indigenous futurity, "consciousness is a rush of shadows in the distance."[4]

As a third example, the U.S. Army began educating Filipino schoolchildren in 1900 as a strategy of conquest in the Philippine–American War. Officers served as school superintendents, enlisted men as teachers, enrolling fifty thousand students in 1904 and

3. Richardson, "Navigating the Problem of Inclusion," 343.
4. Vizenor, quoted ibid., 341.

more than one million in 1935. Colonial schools were considered part of military operations, serving a strategic purpose in quelling resistance. In *The Miseducation of the Filipino,* Renato Constantino asserts, "Education, therefore, serves as a weapon in wars of colonial conquest."[5]

But like the graduates of the boarding schools of Kenya, many of the graduates of these colonial schools defied the schools' intended purpose of making colonial middle management by coming to the United States—exploiting the unintended loophole that colonized Filipinos were U.S. nationals. As Veta Schlimgen explains,

> the desires and ambitions cultivated in the "culture of education" created a new—and unanticipated—(im)migration dynamic when, during the 1920s, Filipino students retraced the steps of American colonizers. They migrated to the mainland states, and they sought college degrees. Filipino student migration during the 1920s increased remarkably. In 1919, about 450 Filipino students studied in the states. Five years later, nearly 2000 did and, in 1930, the number of enrolled students hovered around 3000. These numbers might seem small to us now but in the context of student migration during the interwar years, they are significant. During the 1920s, Filipino students constituted about twenty percent of non-native born students.[6]

Furthermore, "during the first half of the 1920s, students (rather than laborers) made up the majority of Filipino migrants to the mainland U.S." This unexpected product of the colonial desiring machine ultimately helped to mobilize history on the side of brown labor unionists in West Coast farms and canneries. Notable organizers within the Cannery Workers' and Farm Laborers' Union were first accomplished students. Victorio Velasco, after earning a degree in journalism, was shunted into cannery work and farm labor in Seattle. He went on to edit Filipino community newspapers

5. Constantino, "Miseducation of the Filipino," 2.
6. Veta Schlimgen, "Filipino Students and the Promises of American Citizenship," paper presented at the annual meeting of the American Historical Association, San Diego, Calif., 2010, 6.

that were critical to creating a collective Filipino workers' political voice. Chris Mensalvas quit law school because, as a U.S. "noncitizen national" from the Philippines, he was prohibited from practicing law. "I spent three years in college and then I went to organize our people on the farms."[7] Trinidad Rojo, who completed his PhD in sociology at Stanford University, became president of the Cannery Workers' and Farm Laborers' Union in 1939. Their work became one root of the United Farm Worker movement best associated with Dolores Huerta and Cesar Chavez.

The technological fact of the matter is that Rojo, Mensalves, Standing Bear, and wa Thiong'o are scyborg, and their flights through the colonial assemblages reveal a warp in the patterning of power. Scyborgs are possible "men" fit for assimilation—the colonial hope is that the whiteness of the normative human can be extended to the very people who were premised as non-human, gender-deviant savages. Thus I have selected these male examples to bring attention to how, upon entry into schooling, they were all already premised as not men. Natives must get haircuts and Western suits; African boys need to be converted into Christian men; even with suits and Christian names, Filipino men were feared as sexual contagions in white working-class society. You can infer how these same masculinizing technologies are appended onto those of you who are not cis-men and how, despite your colonial equipment, you will never become a complete colonialist stud. The first world university wants you to become masculine in the most disciplined sense of the word and will provide you with the necessary prosthesis and will cut off your tail. But you, as scyborg, might use these technologies to bend the fabric of power to suit your decolonial desires.

Are you scyborg? is not an ontological question. It is a technological reality. In formulating the scyborg, I am attempting to con-

7. Ibid., 12.

nect the person—the being—with the web of intentions beyond the being. In a crude sense, I am connecting agency and structure—although I despise that duality.

Structure as a term by itself has useful explanatory value. I see structure as a limited analytic about how power works. I see agency as a discourse preoccupied with individual freedom within a structuralist analysis. To be sure, there are theorizations of agency that do not participate in this preoccupation, ones that theorize agency as a capacity for action that is enabled by systems. However, I am problematizing the general usage of the term *agency* as a hopeful signifier for resistance. Such positioning is an individualistic theory of change, wherein collective agency is relegated to a mass of individuals operating in unison. That kind of "collective" springs from a theory of individuals.[8] By contrast, the scyborg springs from assemblage. To speak of scyborgs as autonomous, unplugged individuals is meaningless. It only makes sense to discuss the scyborg as plugged in to technological grids. The scyborg is inherently a plurality and only occasionally becomes singular when a condensation of machines

8. Arguably, Hardt and Negri's reclaiming of the multitudes as a model of resistance benefits from this commonsense conceptualization of marginalized individuality as the basis for an autonomous democracy not rooted in the State. Michael Hardt and Antonio Negri, *Multitude: War and Democracy in the Age of Empire* (New York: Penguin, 2005). Their claim is highly problematic when considering the ways that the racial Other is formative of the individual self and the racial is a paradigm that quickly disrupts the equality of marginality from which multitudes arise. Furthermore, Indigenous concepts of the collective first person plural do not assimilate easily into this notion of the multitudes, even though Hardt and Negri essentially use indigeneity as a kind of referent for autonomous groups. For critiques of multitudes, see Elizabeth Maddock Dillon, *New World Drama: The Performative Commons in the Atlantic World, 1649–1849* (Durham, N.C.: Duke University Press, 2014), and Richard J. F. Day and Nick Montgomery, "Letter to a Greek Anarchist: On Multitudes, Peoples, and New Empires," in *Radical Democracy and Collective Movements Today: The Biopolitics of the Multitude versus the Hegemony of the People*, ed. Alexandros Kioupkiolis and Giorgos Katsambekis, 45–72 (New York: Routledge, 2016).

produces intentionality—hopefully a decolonial intentionality, such as a third world university. Fortunately, the decolonial spirit is also personal, and it does not always await a mass mobilization or an ignited fire of the people (as anticolonial revolution is often portrayed). It happens at the scales of cells, tissues, organs, rhizomes—it is the person and the transpersonal. It is always happening. So conceptualized, the scyborg may be personal in scale but is wired into telescoping scales of the assemblage.

In considering the plugged-in scyborg, I am drawing from foundational femtech thinkers who established how the cyborgian body extends beyond the organic boundaries of the person: for example, when you troll someone online, your agential self extends well beyond your skin, across space and beyond corporeality, via your plugs in technological assemblages. Furthermore, "self" is not only extended by technology but can also be divided, fractured, and tapped by it—as in the case of disaggregating the fetus from the mother and womb through ultrasound, or in transnational surrogacy, call centers, and the technology-assisted ways that Global South people's vital energies are sapped and redistributed to support the lives of the Global North.[9]

So the scyborg for me, as a "being" who is only analytically meaningful when we consider your entanglements in the machinery of assemblages, is a fitting way to discuss structural agency.[10] The scyborg is a being who is in no way discretely individual. A scyborg is a being in assemblage. Your agential capacity extends beyond your being, into the system's capacity. Your agency is system. This is why I put the *s* in front of *cyborg*.

9. For femtech, see Haraway, *Simians, Cyborgs, and Women*; for ultrasound, see Barad, "Getting Real"; Vora, *Life Support*.

10. It is a linguistic accident that *agency* has a similar spelling to the French word for "assemblage": *agencement* or "layout; organization." *Agencement* is the term that Deleuze and Guattari used, which became translated into English as "assemblage."

Scyborg is not an identity. Although I am addressing you, as scyborg, I understand that you are a very plural group of beings. Being scyborg does not describe your total reality. Scyborgs are not total beings, nor whole beings, nor perfectly discrete beings for that matter. Scyborg is not ontological. *Scyborg* is more like an adjective.[11] It describes a technological condition of being embedded in an assemblage of machines. Different scyborgs have different powers in shaping assemblage. What your particular powers are is important for you to figure out. Certainly most of us are scyborg, but of particular interest to me is the scyborg who is embedded in the university, who assembles decolonial machines.

The university is in assemblage. One might consider how (1) the university is an assemblage. It is a giant machine composed of myriad working parts, multiple systems. Each part can still be thought of as a discrete organism to be unplugged and replugged somewhere else. (2) The university is *in* assemblage.[12] It is imbricated with other assemblages. The university assemblage is connected to the military–industrial complex, itself another assemblage. At

11. In calling *scyborg* an adjective, I note that scyborg should not be a new sexy identity that displaces critical interrogations about race, gender, sexuality, ability. Here I deviate a bit from Haraway's important writings in *Simians, Cyborgs, and Women* and draw from insights from Jasbir Puar's critique of the binary postulated by the juxtaposition of cyborg and goddess in "I Would Rather Be a Cyborg than a Goddess."

12. In using the phrase "in assemblage" rather than "an assemblage," I am building off of Puar's insights. Puar, "I Would Rather Be a Cyborg than a Goddess"; see also John Phillips, "Agencement/Assemblage," *Theory, Culture, and Society* 23, no. 2–3 (2006): 108–9. "'Assemblage' is actually an awkward translation—the original term in Deleuze and Guattari's work is not the French word *assemblage,* but actually *agencement,* a term which means design, layout, organization, arrangement, and relations—the focus being not on content but on relations, relations of patterns" (57). However, I in effect mean both "universities are an assemblage" and that they are "in assemblage," the latter emphasizing what university scyborgs in assemblage can do as a result of these relations in which they are embedded.

my university, UC San Diego, we have particularly intimate connections with the U.S. Navy. One can easily see how the military–industrial and academic–industrial complexes are in assemblage in terms of engineering contracts with the military; the ways that anthropologists might be recruited to serve as cultural consultants for the military; or how Arabic- and Farsi-speaking undergraduates are actively recruited by the CIA. The university is in assemblage with other corporate capitalist assemblages, such as pharmaceutical and high-tech industries. It is, like all assemblages, discrete from yet amalgamated with other assemblages in an endless matrix of couplings. (3) As assemblages, the priorities of "scale," as captured in the conventional hierarchical dichotomies of micro versus macro, historical versus ephemeral, data versus anecdote, echo into one another. So a small glimpse into a university classroom very quickly telescopes into scales of heterosexism, racial capitalism, and so on. The webs of pedagogical machinery are at once giant and intimate. It may feel like lying face down on a monumental precipice, close enough to see the cracks in the stone as well as the chasm just centimeters away. I think this is why some scyborgs feel vertigo in the college classroom.

Your vertigo is your intuition speaking. You are sensing how power "in your face" is jointed to global latticeworks of power. As Simon Leung reminds us, state-legitimated force is felt at the scale of the visage and the viscera: "The look of law: It's on your face. It's on your case. It's down your throat. It's up your ass. That is, if your ass has not been rendered to disappear altogether."[13] Julie Burelle notes that "moments of vertiginous consciousness" are these sudden apprehensions of the fatal couplings of the personal and structural scales: "a sensation of sudden clarity, a sinking of the solar plexus if you will, about the violence that continues to hold one's settler-colonial privilege in place."[14]

13. Simon Leung, "The Look of Law," *Art Journal* 66, no. 3 (2007): 38.
14. Julie Burelle, "Theatre in Contested Lands: Repatriating Indigenous Remains," *The Drama Review* 59, no. 1 (2015): 116.

Ruth Wilson Gilmore pushes us to analyze the geographies of these "fatal couplings of power and difference" as multiscalar. For Gilmore, the "warfare state is also the racial-gendered state," as the industrial killings of racialized enemy others are jointed to the domestication of racial-gendered industries within the state. Thus who you are is not at all distant from power that is exercised on bodies and lands geographically distant from your body. The goal is "to figure out what [and who] makes oppressive and liberatory structures work, and what [and who] makes them fall apart."[15] Just as Gilmore seeks a multiscalar object of analysis, I seek a multiscalar subject of power.[16] Scyborg agency is multiscalar; the witch's flight is the ripple in the patterning of power.

The scyborg's medium is assemblage. When we take assemblages seriously as both analytical of power and as the medium for it, then the question becomes, how do you hack assemblages? The scyborg is a sculptor of assemblage[17]—s-he splices one machine to another, de/links apparatuses from/to one another, places machines to work in making new machines, disassembles and reassembles the machine. The scyborg can connect Black radical thought to the paper-producing academic–industrial complex and set the print command to "manifesto." The scyborg is like R2D2 in the Death Star, opening escape tunnels, lowering and raising

15. Ruth Wilson Gilmore, "Fatal Couplings of Power and Difference: Notes on Racism and Geography," *The Professional Geographer* 54, no. 1 (2002): 21.

16. I am using subject here to include a person (the scyborg) who is interpellated in lattices of power (the scyborg is at once subjugated by power, produced as a subject by power, and a subjective participant in power) but also the wills, forces, and desires that surround and exceed a person (the scyborg in assemblage). The scyborg is a who/what that powers multiscalar dynamics in lattices of power.

17. It is yet another linguistic accident that *assemblage* seems to reference "assemblage," meaning "collage" in avant-garde art. However, collage is an incomplete metaphor.

doors to new passageways, making the death machine run backward, and ultimately releasing the plans for its destruction.[18] The scyborg is an artist in the un/patterning of relations of power.[19]

The scyborg loves dirty work.[20] Scyborgs do not care whether the assemblage they are retooling is first, second, or third world. Categorical thinking is not the point. Nothing is too dirty for scyborg dreaming: MBA programs, transnational capital, Department of Defense grants. Scyborgs are ideology-agnostic, which creates possibilities in every direction of the witch's flight—not just possibilities that we like. This is why some of you are not always decolonial in behavior. Thankfully, your newly assembled machine will break down. Some other scyborgs will reassemble the busted gears to drive decolonial dreams. To dream it is to ride the ruin.

18. Yet, this is to say, the scyborg is not an individual robot. The scyborg is your personal influence in a far larger robot. Here I am talking about the collective agency of your decolonial machine.

19. In a Gramscian sense, the scyborg is an "inorganic" intellectual.

20. "What is the ideology of an assemblage?" is a question that makes sense only in broken ways. First, ideology makes sense in terms of the intention of the design; and ideology makes sense in terms of what the assemblage actually produces; and ideology makes sense in terms of ideological material that is scattered about the assemblage. Each of these senses is broken. The actual assemblage always breaks from the intended design (and we can think of examples like Indian boarding schools, on one hand—they did not succeed wholly in exterminating Native peoples—and, on the other, revolutionary nationalisms, which did not succeed in liberating the people from oppressive patriarchal states). Real production is the result of real machines that are always breaking down. See Gilles Deleuze and Félix Guattari, *Anti-Oedipus: Capitalism and Schizophrenia,* trans. Robert Hurley, Mark Seem, and Helen R. Lane (Minneapolis: University of Minnesota Press, 1983). Ideological material is impure; ideas and ideologies are also scavenger materials that are woven together to build new assemblages. In the art of assemblages, the question of ideology cannot be fixed to the objects in assemblage—a point with which I might differ from certain views in the STS debate. What the assemblage actually produces is a kind of practical ideology—and this is what the assemblage produces when it breaks down (and in D&G+F formulation, all machines are breaking down; they work by breaking down). A critical discussion of ideology can only be done by talking about ideological breakage.

Scyborgs are creating the free university. Scyborg desires are connecting the neoliberal motor that drove President Obama's campaign for tuition-free community college to antipoverty organizing and to critical education. One of the interesting ways this is being done is by connecting free universities to the rhetoric of democracy and citizenship. Democracy is not decolonization. Democratization will expand, at best, the normative class of citizens through reinvestments in settler colonialism and new articulations of antiblackness. However, "democracy" as a discourse was also ready material for assemblage, a gear to attach to build the free university. The dream of universal education is born from the reality of exclusive schooling. This dream may shift as educational expansion creates new imbalances, such as inflated credentials, the devaluing of unschooled knowledge, new gaps between educational training and employment, or gaps between the trained workforce and the available supply of jobs. However, in building the free university assemblage and watching it fall apart, perhaps something unpredictable will come of its ruin. As to what, and whether the free university will be decolonizing, will be answered in scyborg assemblage.

To be very clear, I am not advocating for rescuing the university from its own neoliberal desires but rather for assembling decolonizing machines, to plug the university into decolonizing assemblages.

Close to my heart, Roses in Concrete Community School opened its doors in 2015 in Ohlone, what some call Oakland, California. This school is part of a larger self-determination project for a mostly Black and Brown community, in which we hope for a pre-K–16 educational institution, community-based economies, and land.[21]

Also in 2015, also in what is now called Oakland, longtime Indigenous educators and activists Corrina Gould (Chochenyo/

21. http://rosesinconcrete.org/.

Karkin Ohlone) and Johnella LaRose (Shoshone Bannock) created the first women-led urban Indigenous land trust built upon "the belief that land is the foundation" that can bring all peoples together in "the return of Chochenyo and Karkin Ohlone lands . . . to Indigenous stewardship." Sogorea Te' Land Trust also reworks Western concepts of "land tax," nonprofit status, and inheritance. Decolonizing land relations is the heart that reworks this machinery. Sogorea Te' not only calls on but indeed provides an avenue for people living in Ohlone lands "to heal from the legacies of colonialism and genocide, to remember different ways of living, and to do the work that our ancestors and future generations are calling us to do."[22]

Nearby Roses in Concrete is an abandoned U.S. Navy base the size of a small town. California community colleges are talking expansion, while the tuition-free college movement had nearly found a federal reality under President Obama. A scyborg might connect these pieces—might imagine how the machines of freedom schools and free community colleges could purchase land, land that could become part of an Indigenous land trust.

Roses in Concrete has a sister school in Aoteroa that originated from a Māori bilingual program Te Whānau o Tupuranga (Centre for Māori Education) and Fanau Pasifika (Centre for Pasifika Education), which became a school in 2006 and then became Kia Aroha College in 2011. Similar to Roses, Kia Aroha College is built on a holistic "scholar warrior" culture that developed the school over twenty-five years into a "culturally-located, bilingual learning model based in a secure cultural identity, stable positive relationships, and aroha (authentic caring and love)."[23] This craft of creating Indigenous space in an urban colonial context requires a constant rearrangement of settler law, Indigenous rights, state

22. http://sogoreate-landtrust.com/.

23. Beverley Ann Milne, "Colouring in the White Spaces: Reclaiming Cultural Identity in Whitestream Schools," PhD diss., University of Waikato, 2013, http://hdl.handle.net/10289/7868.

educational ministry systems, built schooling environments, and community systems of Indigenous education. Furthermore, these associations between school makers in Māori/Pasifika and in U.S. ghetto colonial contexts produce new shared scyborg flight plans. These technologies are driven and repurposed by scyborg desires.

Where I am now, on Kumeyaay land at UC San Diego, we are at the confluence of the engineering apparatus, the naval and sea industries, the U.S.–Mexican border, the white utopian project of Black exclusion, the settler project of Native disappearance, the transnational project of international (read model Asian) recruitment. Scyborgs might reorganize these technologies into third university organisms with decolonizing programs: a project of water, a project of transnational/Indigenous solidarity, a project of Black assertion, a project of islands.

As I write, Eve Tuck and K. Wayne Yang (my other I) are supporting a collective of collectives, the Land Relationships Super Collective, that connects different land-based movements across North America with one another to share strategies, resources, learnings, and so on. As Eve and I are both university professors, the university plays into this as an institution that must be refused, and yet also as an organism, an assemblage of machines, that we can make work, make space in, make liquid enough to allow us to contribute to land rematriation projects directly.

The third world university will be built by scyborg labor. This is not a revolutionary call for scyborgs of the world to unite. This is a call to gear-in and do the dirty work of desiring machines. Through desires' dirty work, we might recommission these first world scraps into a third world machine.

A Scyborg Commencement

It is a technological fact that you are scyborg. As such, you permeate the system; your capacities are system; and depending on what femtech powers you might be able to access, you have some influence over what assemblages do. You as scyborg are not the only agentive body in assemblage. There are other sculptors, and assemblages themselves will act however and do whatever they please. However, the scyborg is *your* agentive body. It is personal. It is a "personal" that operates from assemblage. You are your own personal scyborg.

You are not just a scyborg. There are other ways to analyze your agency. You could also be a monster, an orphan, a ghost. You might jump scale.[24] You might cut and break.[25] Your scyborg agency does not preclude the other choices that you have. In whatever case, you are a disturbance in the electromagnetic field. I see your shimmering outline.

You as scyborg are constructed in assemblage, and you are interpellated by assemblage, and yet you can also operate through the university and other assemblages because of some of its technologies that you appropriate. This technological condition is only sensible within assemblage. Should you graduate or get expelled or get unplugged, you would no longer be scyborg in the same ways (without the same technological powers, without the same access to the matrix of technologies). Scyborg is an impermanent condition. Technologies change. Technological beings become obsolete. Try to be restful when you finally reach that junk heap.

Scyborgs are part machine and part ghost. Scyborgs gain an inheritance from the university at the price exacted upon their body, their kin, and their future—paid in blood and in kinship and in unpayable debt. This is not poetry—this is the student debt, the mortgage of the family home, the disowning and disavowal of the student by hir community, the obligation to become something successful and skillful and seductive.

If you are a student, you accrue other forms of debt besides student loans. Signithia Fordham talks about "Black children's suc-

24. Karyn Recollet, "Gesturing Indigenous Futurities through the Remix," *Dance Research Journal* 48, no. 1 (2016): 91–105.

25. Stefano Harney and Fred Moten, *The Undercommons: Fugitive Planning and Black Study* (New York: Minor Compositions, 2013).

cess in school as conferring the burden of acting white. It is indeed a burden."[26] Some people will only envy your school-issued rocket boots and comment on how much you've changed—which is a coded insult for how much you have forgotten, even if you have not.

Scyborgs inherit a lot and a load. Therefore scyborgs are not inherently decolonial. The scyborg hirself has a chance at freedom, that is, at freedom's doppelganger—a lot of land, a bit of wealth, a right to rights. The scyborg might be foolish not to reach for this mirage of freedom.

There is no freedom in the scyborg. It is not a liberated figure. Scyborgs are privileged. Scyborgs are technologically enhanced colonial subjects. This is not a scyborg manifesto.

It's not so bad. The scyborg carries the third world university in hir gears, and the fourth world in hir soul.

I have a scyborg friend; perhaps I have more than one. Once we planned Earthseed together. Once we built a freedom school together. Once again, you build it. One day, you will build another Black life center. Once more, we talk about your community college, and your Black Star solar company and planting solar forests in asphalt schoolyards, and jobs for (y)our communities. One another, we augment each other's scyborg powers. One and others, scyborg dreams become blueprints, become realities, become ruins, become soil for scyborg schemes. Only the bad guys build things that last forever. Scyborg friend, another world is dreaming your dreams.

26. Signithia Fordham, "What Does an Umbrella Do for the Rain? On the Efficacy and Limitations of Resistance," in Tuck and Yang, *Youth Resistance Research and Theories of Change*, 98.

Acknowledgments

I WOULD LIKE TO THANK the organizers with decolonizing desires in the university whose paths have met with mine, including the blade-bearing residents of the Undercommons, especially we who remember 2010; Monsters, Orphans, Robots; *At least we look good*; Amunraw and Black renaissance in Shanghai; organizers who have returned to UCSD; Some of you are ghost-writing this book, some are ghost-riding this book. The organizers and participants of the Decolonizing the University Conference and of the Harvard Student of Color Conference, 2010, your *encuentros* helped to foment these writings into a book. A Black Studies Project and the Militarisms and Migrations Institute (whenever you will exist) remind me of the organic, living, noncybernetic matters of this work. Thank you Angie Morrill, Eve Tuck, Curtis Marez, and C. Ree. This wouldn't have made it to print without your affirmations and criticisms. Special thanks to Noelani Goodyear-Ka'ōpua, for your generous feedback, which directed me to think more deeply about the metaphor of cinema and the importance of collective agency, and also lessened many of the flaws of this final version. Kamala Visweswaran and the Department of Ethnic Studies at UC San Diego, thank you for creating a small colloquium to discuss this book. Thank you to my very encouraging editor, Danielle Kasprzak, and to Anne Carter and editors behind the scenes at the University of Minnesota Press who shepherded this manuscript to publication. Finally, thank you, C. Ree, for gifting me my best ideas and for making this done.

la paperson is also K. Wayne Yang, who writes about decolonization and everyday epic organizing, often with frequent collaborator Eve Tuck. Together they authored the widely read essay "Decolonization Is Not a Metaphor." la paperson's writings include "The Postcolonial Ghetto" and "A Ghetto Land Pedagogy: An Antidote for Settler Environmentalism." S-he is working on a forthcoming book about deep organizing.